KEY WORDS

The Impact On Bible Translation

KEY WORDS

The Impact On Bible Translation

DAN KRAMER

XULON PRESS

Xulon Press
2301 Lucien Way #415
Maitland, FL 32751
407.339.4217
www.xulonpress.com

© 2020 by Dan Kramer

Printed in the United States of America.

PAPERBACK ISBN-13: 978-1-63221-150-7

EBOOK ISBN-13: 978-1-63221-151-4

Table of Contents

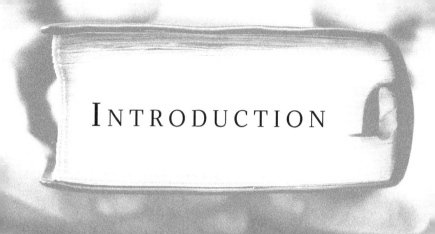

INTRODUCTION

> "I'd rather strive for the kind of inter-
> view where instead of me asking to
> introduce myself to society, society asks
> me to introduce myself to society."
> — Criss Jami, Killosophy

I've resisted doing this. I fear acknowledgment
and desire nothing. I hope for the impact of others
to glean something of use. I am and will always be
a teacher.

I hope to coordinate this book with a workbook in
the future, so I can help empower readers to translate
the Bible for themselves. I have been greatly encouraged to tell the story of MAST and while that is a great
story, it is God's story. It continues to unfold in unbe-
lievable ways.

This book is written in layers. Educational layers
exist to provoke thought and take you somewhere.
Individual pieces, but also the whole picture exist in
layers as well. They are surrounded by key words. In
writing this, I had to ask, "What are the key words I
would focus on to express how the MAST movement
happened?" If this could be taken and further owned

by the readers, then they understand what to do with it, perhaps far beyond me.

The layers of these chapters, for the most part, include a title, thoughtful quote, a key word, and a reflection on the key word.

Language changes over time. The use of a dictionary has significantly decreased due to the rise of Google. This change, over time, is a linguistic principle that cries out the need of ownership being a key component of Bible translation. As we hope to see Bible poverty eradicated around the world, we hope it never returns again. The only sense to that hope is through giving this task away. The only audience to give it to who can possibly manage it is the Church.

CHAPTER ONE
I Will Carry Your Bags

"As long as you are proud you cannot know God. A proud man is always looking down on things and people: and, of course, as long as you are looking down you cannot see something that is above you."
— **C.S. Lewis,** *Mere Christianity*

Key Word: Humility

Webster 1828 defines "humility" as: In ethics, freedom from pride and arrogance, humbleness of mind; a modest estimate of one's own worth. In theology, humility consists in lowliness of mind; a deep sense of one's own unworthiness in the sight of God, self-abasement, penitence for sin, and submission to the divine will.

Google 2020: a modest or low view of one's own importance; humbleness

Noted Changes:
- No reference to arrogance
- "Freedom from pride"
- Worth vs importance
- Lowliness of mind
- Unworthiness in the sight of God
- No reference to sin
- No reference to submission
- No reference to divine will

Location: India 2011 and 2014

"Why do we get to do this?" Mike Hatfield asked as we stood in the middle of a room of nearly two hundred people who spoke thirty different languages. We were just outside of Bangalore, India. Mike, my former pastor, now worked for me. At the time, I didn't have an answer. I pushed out a distant thought. "I don't know," I answered.

"Why hasn't someone else thought of this?" Mike asked. He was referring to a new methodology for Bible translation that we were implementing for the first time in India. The methodology, known as MAST (Mobilized Assistance Supporting Translation), was being tested by two established Bible translation organizations in India. As we were surrounded and observed for everything we did, all I could do was reflect on the history Mike and I shared in ministry.

Three years prior to that meeting in India, I personally met Mike by accident. I had just moved to a new city and settled into a church, and I made it a point to reach out to the pastor of missions. I had begun a new life, trading a teaching career for the mission field. When I arrived for a scheduled lunch with the pastor,

Mike greeted me and said the pastor was ill, but he was glad to go out to lunch with me and hear about the ministry I was engaged in. We went to a tiny restaurant and I shared about the ministry. At that time, the ministry was providing English as a second language (ESL) programs to Bible translators so they could become more functional in their roles. After a half hour into the conversation, Mike expressed that he would love to see the ministry. "I'd just like to go and carry your bags so I could see it!" Mike said.

I was struck by the humility of his statement. I had always grown up with a reverence for the role of pastors, so I couldn't imagine a pastor carrying my bags for me, let alone taking time out of his busy schedule to see what I do.

"So let's go!" I responded.

Mike did go with me to India, as well as Nepal, and little did we know that the circumstances of the trip would bond us in ways we could never have predicted. From cancelled flights to explorations of new cities to seeing our personality differences play out in certain situations, we became quick friends. Of all the experiences over those few days of travel, there was one moment that made me stop; it planted something in me forever.

Mike and I had finally made it out of India and into Kathmandu, Nepal. We met with a Bible translation partner and heard about the ministry over the decades. The meeting was a few hours long, then Mike and I began our walk back to the city. As we did, Mike fell a few steps behind me. I looked back and he was actually standing still, a bit choked up. I don't know if I said anything, but I could hear in his voice that God had touched him. "People don't know," Mike said. "That right there was the Great Commission, and no one ever sees that!" From that moment, Mike began to transition toward a role that only God could design. Mike began serving in our English program, but more importantly, he became a key staff member on our Education Services team for Wycliffe Associates.

A few years later, and filled with a whole lot of life changes and experiences, Mike asked: "Why do we get to do this?" and "Why hasn't someone else thought of this?" We found ourselves standing before leaders of organizations we were already serving through ESL, and we had the opportunity to lead them in teaching a new method for Bible translation. Who were *we* to do such a thing?

I reflected on the question, then I reflected on that question for Mike. All I could say was, "I think it is because our team has always practiced godly humility and He knew we would follow Him through the task He gave us."

BIBLICAL FOUNDATION: 1 PETER 5

There are a lot of passages that mention "humility" in the Bible. It is woven throughout Scripture. Through Jesus arrival alone, humility is expressed. It is demonstrated throughout Jesus' earthly life. We could reflect on people, including Moses when he asked, "Who am I?" and David's reflection on how God was mindful of him, widows, warriors, prophets, and judges. We can also look at the antithesis of humility in the traits of arrogance and pride, which were at the center of Satan's temptation of Adam and Eve in the garden. Of all the examples and perspectives, however, Peter cuts to the core of the battle between pride and humility.

Peter was the bold man who leapt out of the boat, pulled his sword to defend his master, and marked forever by the fate that he would deny knowing Jesus. The inward battle between humility and pride existed in Peter and it seems he came to terms with it years after his denial.

I remember glimpses of Scripture as a child. One of those moments was the visual description of a prowling lion waiting to devour (1 Pet. 5:8). That image easily engaged my mind and was both exciting as a story and terrifying as a personal image. The verse expresses that we should resist the prowling lion. As a boy, I asked "Um, how?" At that time, the cherry-picked reference to the verse didn't afford me any insights. As an adult, the message of the verse is different because I read the context of the whole chapter. The answer to the "how" shocked me. We are simply to be humble.

In 1 Peter 5, Peter referred to the church and the church elders. Keeping in mind that the church was relatively young, "elders" was also a relative term in what we might think of today in our key words. The chapter talks about shepherding in the early verses and later gets to the seriousness of what the church was to prepare its flock for—the prowling lion.

First, let's think about the purpose of shepherding others. If there is ever a role that could lead to a sense of pride, it is when someone holds knowledge and training over another person. Second, if a person is training another in the foundation of faith and building a church, what exactly are those traits that combat the prowling lion? Who better than Peter, who struggled with his sense of self-worth, prideful boldness, and failure, to give us insights into a better approach?

The traits became clear as Peter exhorted the elders to shepherd the flock. Willingness over duty (verse 1), not seeking gain (verse 2), eager (verse 2), not dominating (verse 3), an example (verse 3), submissive (verse 5), clothed in humility (verse 5). God opposes the proud (verse 5), giving grace to the humble (verse 5); therefore, humble yourself (verse 6), give God your anxiety (verse 7). There are eleven traits and three directly express the word "humility." One expresses the opposite of humility as bad and the other seven need humility in their functioning.

Keep in mind, this came from Peter who lived a life of working through the traits to overcome in his task of building the foundation of the Church. This is a recipe from a person that should be noted for all of us.

MAST METHODOLOGY

MAST methodology was born out of a request from Jeewan, the son of a Bible translator. He asked if I could help create a method that assisted Bible translation better for his people. My interpretation of that included three things. The first included an increased ownership for national Bible translators. The second, a new methodology needed to be faster so Jeewan could see the change in people, communities, and the nation that his heart desired. Finally, I sensed that there was a need of restoration. Meaning, it was actually a joy to do the work and not an isolated laborious task over a long period of time.

Before anything could be done, I believed with all my heart that a sense of humility in the conversation had to be present. There was a desperate ask and setting aside of pride in the history of the work that had already been done. There was a definite answer of humility with the sense of "Who am I?" but further "Does this help?" as things unfolded in conversations of dual submissiveness.

A team that developed an English language learning program that was second to none evolved MAST into what it is now. This program far out-paced the research in language acquisition and served Bible translation well. The team that facilitated the program across thirty nations referred to it as "the nameless and faceless program." In other words, there was no credit, no publishing, no profit, and no gain. It was purely for the students to grow and excel. That same team, and its sense of humility, laid the foundation for MAST. For those seeking to participate in MAST at any level—facilitator, translator, organizer, observer, critical evaluator, or support for any given need—humility will lend to success in regard to what God wants to do. Humility will grow each individual through the process. Without it, we fail.

ANALYSIS OF KEY WORDS

In the definitions at the beginning of this chapter, look at what is missing over the time span in our culture. Then ask yourself: Does the absence of these words help or hurt society? Is the absence of reflecting on these words helping or hurting me? Would the inclusion of these words and the reflection of what they mean be beneficial in how we evaluate our humility? Does our current definition impact how we treat this quality in our lives?

A Look at Key(ed) Words

Just before MAST was developed, as we were running English programs in India which Mike was leading, he was offered a wider opportunity of role and management. A couple of emails between Mike and me demonstrate the humility Mike had, even as the opportunity was offered.

On May 14, 2014, at 12:55 AM, "Dan Kramer" <dan_ kramer@wycliffeassociates.org> wrote:

Hello from sunny Orlando! I started writing you a novel of an email and thought—not now. So let me put it into one question (two parts):

How would you feel about being the complete Asia ELL Coordinator? If you are feeling "the call" (because I know you're capable of not only managing it, but growing it), I'll follow-up with a giant email with details, but I would start to initiate this with you and then others so when we meet in Nepal we can use the "extra time" to really put it all together solidly. What are your thoughts?

Dan

Response from Mike:

Wow... It's 6:20am. Just reading over all your email! Wow... God is really working!! I love the thoughts... Sounds amazing. Let me wake up, and as I can today, I'll send some thoughts and questions. Starting some presentations today! What a quality group of students. Amazing...!

In awe... Mike

On May 14, 2014, at 11:21 PM, "Dan Kramer" <dan_kramer@wycliffeassociates.org> wrote:

Here we go....:) First, aside from your story, the overall picture (in the rear-view mirror) of seeing God's timing is always amazing to me. So what do I see? In past perspective, where was the leading—India. What (all in timing that coordinated with you and life events) happened in India? Nothing short of amazing.

Response from Mike:

Wow... Praying about this before I answer. I'll send some thoughts and questions as I form them a little better than my early morning thinking right now. :-)

Having dinner with (India Bible Translation Leader) tomorrow night at his home. I think he is sold on ELL. We will see what he is thinking. Students continue to excel! Wow... This stuff works!!

Hope u r doing great... Mike

Humility Traits Demonstrated: First reactions—awe of what God is doing, time for prayer, sense of others. What wasn't shown: pride in accomplishment, sense of entitlement, questions about self-interests.

CHAPTER TWO

Prepared and Ready for Loss

"Every now and then I like to do as I'm
told, just to confuse people."
— **Tamora Pierce,** *Melting Stones*

Key Word: Obedience

Webster 1828: Compliance with a command, prohibition or known law and rule of duty prescribed; the performance of what is required or enjoined by authority, or the abstaining from what is prohibited, in compliance with the command or prohibition. To constitute obedience the act or forbearance to act must be in submission to authority; the command must be known to the person, and his compliance must be in consequence of it; or it is not obedience. Obedience is not synonymous with obsequiousness; the latter often implying meanness or servility, and obedience being merely a proper submission to authority. That which duty requires implies dignity of conduct rather than servility. Obedience may be voluntary or involuntary. Voluntary obedience alone can be acceptable by God.

Google 2020: Compliance with an order, request, or law or submission to another's authority.

Noted Changes:

- Command vs order
- No mention of prohibition, duty, performance, enjoined, abstaining
- Distinction between known and unknown (obsequiousness)
- Dignity vs servility
- Voluntary/involuntary
- No mention of God

Location: Orlando, Florida. A meeting room with Bruce Smith, the kitchen table (2013) and the streets of Nepal (2014).

"Did he hear me?" I thought as I presented a brilliant question in my slide show for Bruce Smith to ponder. It wasn't often that I got to meet with Bruce. He was the CEO of Wycliffe Associates. In fact, besides the casual hallway greetings and encounters, this was only my second formal meeting with him. Brent Ropp, the Vice President of Operations, was also in the meeting. I was included so I could review the English Language Learning (ELL) programs that had spread around the world over the last four years. They spread so successfully that they started to dominate the activity of the organization in ways that triggered questions for Bruce in terms of prioritization of impact on Bible translation. He was wondering, despite the success and praise of others who wanted the program, "Is this the best use of our resources?"

At first, as this meeting was scheduled, I was nervous about what would happen. In the language programs we provided, relationships often became very personal as we saw the growth of the students over months and years. I had wondered, "What will happen to these programs and what relationships might be severed if we cut back?" After some time, I began approaching the meeting more prayerfully and even with anticipation as I thought, "This is an opportunity to serve my leadership right to the top."

I have often noticed in my life, that when I make the effort to align myself according to what I know is true, other opportunities open up, including unexpected blessings.

Between the time I was notified of the meeting so I could review the programs under my management to the time of the actual meeting, Jeewan approached me about assisting Nepal in a new methodology for Bible translation. This was a very short window to do many things. First, I had to contact Brent to see if I was allowed to pursue serving a partner that way within my role. Second, I needed to learn. I had no idea how to respond to Jeewan's question. I asked him to provide me with everything he could to show me what they were doing to accomplish Bible translation. He did so quickly. Finally, I had to put some thoughts together on what a potential program would look like if we were going to do something. I didn't want to approach the leaders of the organization and ask the question with no solution in mind. I wanted to proactively serve the request because I deeply cared for Jeewan. In short, I wanted to seek the opportunity with the support of leadership, but I knew it was their decision to make.

During the two weeks before my meeting, I was extremely busy with an English program we facilitated in Orlando. Departmentally, we called the program "The Circus" because three rings of activity always took place at the same time, including host family coordination, teaching, and the underlying logistics of food, transportation, and activities. I found myself preparing for the meeting with Bruce and Brent the night before by reviewing everything Jeewan sent me. I tried to put something together that could provide the support he asked for—at least in concept. At my kitchen table, after all the kids went to bed, I scribbled out the process of Bible translation in Nepal according to what Jeewan described to me. I tried to put it in stages, timelines, and compartments that made sense from a teaching position. I had a decent amount of linguistics in my own education, so I understood the concepts enough and respected the knowledge over the decades of what Bible translation had accomplished. I found myself asking again, "*Who am I* to offer something up to this group doing such a great work of God?"

I called Jeewan that night to ask more questions. Then I offered up possible ways we might help. He politely expressed encouragement, but I could tell it wasn't really what he was hoping for. I hung up feeling exhausted and deflated, so I decided to go to bed.

As I left the dining room, I looked back at the paper I had scribbled on and I saw one small phrase: church checking, six months later. In Nepal, after drafting text, it was taken to the church that speaks the language for feedback from the community. I asked myself, "What if I were the translator (student), and I didn't get my work checked for six months? How would I feel?"

God whispered to my heart. "Start with what you know," He said. I sat back down and thought as a teacher. I could hear Him in what I wrote out, acknowledging that I needed to be who I was and not try to be someone I wasn't. In other words, God made me a teacher, so I had to answer the question as a teacher, not a linguist.

The next morning, I took my scribbled papers to Jeewan and only had two minutes to show him what I had. He immediately said, "Yes! That's what we want!" I stared back at him in disbelief and he stood steady, looking back at me. I went to the meeting with Bruce, slideshow ready, with one slide in the middle of my program review that read, "A Bible translation partner in Nepal has asked if we can create a New Bible translation methodology. Can we pilot a trial program in 2014?"

What I didn't realize is, Bruce hears just about everything and is extremely perceptive. He reserved his response to my question until I finished my entire presentation. I dare not quote him directly because we have a six-year dispute over what I'm sure I heard and what he thinks he said. So I will paraphrase. He told me with very encouraging words to go forward with the experiment in Nepal and to meet with others in collaboration. He further encouraged me by saying that I should spare no expense in doing so. Now, despite his argument and denial to that second statement even to the point of trying to reference a heritage of frugality, we have determined that we will resolve this issue in heaven. If I am correct, he will be my personal pilot for a millennia. Okay, he hasn't agreed to that (yet), but let me offer it here as a heavenly wager.

BIBLICAL FOUNDATION: GENESIS 11, ACTS 2, REVELATION 7

The 1828 definition of obedience at the beginning of the chapter has an amazing amount of depth to explore. It is stunning to see the reflections the dictionary had about God within such words. In Scripture, obedience is a fascinating journey that perplexes in big and small ways. In the larger sense, we see obedience as a societal issue when Israel went through cycles of sin, occupation, and various forms of leadership. We can also see societies' obedience/disobedience in passages that refer to kings, tribes, and events, including the destruction of Sodom and Gomorrah, the plagues in Egypt, the Great Flood, and the Tower of Babel. All these people, cultures, and places were impacted by their obedience, or lack thereof, to God.

The 1828 definition of obedience notes the choice we have within that. We can see instances of disobedience. Jonah doesn't go, Pharaoh doesn't release and those in Babel don't disperse. Today, we live by simpler definitions. Compliance and submission to authority is a common understanding of obedience today. Is that really what is desired by God? Is that what was desired in Babel?

For a second, think of language as a tool for obedience. It may sound strange to think of needing a tool for obedience, but this is often the case. For Noah, the tool was an ark. For Adam and Eve, it was resisting the fruit. For some it was a sacrifice, a temple, or a symbolic element given by God. For others it was a sword, a crown, or a prophetic dream. God calls on us to use what we have when He wants us to use it.

What about language? In this sense, we had a gift back in Babel—a common language. It was a gift that was not understood, appreciated, or perhaps even acknowledged. That is, until the language changed. Once it changed, obedience came into reality. The message was received—whether wanted or not—to disperse. What did God want? Was it separation, isolation, and distance? And was the action of obedience/disobedience and forced confusion leading to dispersed people groups really justified? If viewed from the authoritative-punitive perspective in this small context, it seems harsh.

Yet, if we look back just a little bit in Genesis, we can reflect differently on what happened. First, we can see that this is an event that is not too long after the destruction of the world, which was caused by an unrighteous disobedience toward God. The only listed event prior to the Tower of Babel is the flood. Some estimate that only a hundred years passed between the flood and Babel. It's worth asking, "Could this command to disperse, from God, be protective in some way to avoid a repeat of disobedience?" Further, we can also see that people did not just resist the command, but they tried to pave their own way forward. They did not just worship falsely, but also made themselves God's replacement. If that is not the heart of disobedience, nothing is. So, what did God use? Language. How is that a tool?

Remember the definition in the 1828 *Webster's Dictionary*. "Obedience may be voluntary or involuntary." Let's make no mistake, however, God's will is well beyond our obedience. God creates the tools, calls for the tools, and even puts the tools in our hands. In Genesis 11, the disobedience of society dishonored

God. Now, language is a tool to disperse and confuse people, but we still have the choice to use it to be obedient and honor Him or not. We see this as a path in Acts 2, which highlights the Day of Pentecost. God shows us again that He is in charge of language. It is His tool and there is a choice to use it for His glory and honor or not. Those who spoke of His testimony did. Those who refused and made fun, did not. In Revelation 7, we see the end of this language journey that started at Babel. It was a time where those who chose obedience in a salvation sense honored and praised God.

It's not language as a tool that I am trying to highlight here, it is obedience. We can use anything God provides to us to demonstrate obedience. When given the opportunity to receive a question for serving a person in Nepal, I had a choice—obedience with what God provided me or not? When Bruce wanted to review my programs and perhaps reprioritize and streamline effectiveness, I had a choice of obedience, meaning resist the authority God placed in Bruce's leadership or willfully offer up all I had, and more, for him to evaluate. Obedience is in all we do with what we are given. Obedience is a willful response of, "Here I am," when God wants to give us what He knows is best.

MAST METHODOLOGY

There have always been two qualities—humility and obedience—expressed to the staff that has facilitated the ELL programs within Wycliffe Associates. Often, obedience is defined through examples of response to God, leadership, opportunities, and the task given. This was not a soft sense of submissiveness; it was a diligent pursuit of honoring God.

In 2014, we held the pilot program for MAST in Nepal, and the team walked back to our temporary home talking about the potential for the program because we saw positive changes happening. Then we asked questions about our English program. We were aware that the notion of the program we loved dearly and had successfully facilitated around the globe for four years was ending. Within the next three months, we finished our commitments. Then, we virtually shut down our entire English Language program across the globe and taught our entire facilitation staff MAST methodology.

We could have tried to hang on to the program we loved. We could have come up with lists of reasons why we still needed to do the program. At the same time, we clearly heard God calling us to do something else and to do it fast. With a diligent obedience, a staff of nearly thirty people gave up the program they loved and redesigned everything they did. That is obedience. That is what God desires in obedience. It wasn't a response in servant-like fashion; it was knowing and believing that God had something better. I believe those at Babel had something better waiting for them, too. They chose not to see their tools or use them in the way God desired. I pray we all have hearts of obedience as this keyword has become morphed and lost in our culture.

As translation occurs all over the world today, the question, "Who am I?" is still asked, and there are choices of obedience. We had two equally important goals within the new program, which created a necessary tension between them—diligently maintaining the process and giving the church full ownership of the project. With the placement of these tools in the hands of the church, obedience is relevant beyond the story of how MAST was born. This story continues in the obedience of thousands of translators who respond to the call. Then, those translators diligently adhere to the process and further integrate the entire effort of translation within their lives. Beyond those efforts, they carry obedience into existence within the church.

ANALYSIS OF KEY WORDS

Is it possible to feel dignity in the midst of obedience? How might that clue us in to how we are misguided in the term at times? When you hear the word "obedience," who do you think of first? Is it God? When you think of the word, do you think of it as a term of love or harshness? What loss have we had in this term over a century and a half? Would you say our society is more like Babel or more like those testifying to God in Acts 2?

A LOOK AT KEY(ED) WORDS

From: Dan Kramer <dan_kramer@wycliffeassociates.org>
Date: October 18, 2013 at 10:17:02 AM EDT
To: Brent Ropp <brent_ropp@wycliffeassociates.org>
Subject: Re: SE Asia Staff Orientation in Chiang Mai, Thailand

Hi Dan,

I know that you are up to your ears in ELL training right now, but **I'm wondering if there will be any time next week that we could get together for a few minutes? I need to talk with you and Paul about a particular issue related to your planning for the upcoming year.**

I'll be in the office next week on Monday – Thursday. I'm out of the office on Friday and I leave Monday for the President's Summit in CA so will be away until November 5.

Thanks for your consideration. If you are unable to get over here to the office next week but could be available for 20-30 minutes sometime at the church where you are holding classes, I'll try to get over to see you. Just let me know what works best.

I'm praying that all is going well for you and the team there this week.

Blessings,

Brent

Dan's Response:

Hi Brent,

Welcome home. I have enough staff and volunteer support to be flexible. I could arrange the following:

- Monday afternoon 12 onward
- Tuesday any time.
- Wednesday is a maybe.
- Thursday is possible in the AM.

All is going well here. If there is anything I can bring to the discussion or plan for, I will. I'll definitely bring my calendar.

Thanks

Dan

On Oct 18, 2013, at 9:49 AM, Brent Ropp Wrote:

Dan,

Please let me know if you **are able to meet with us**

on Thursday, Nov. 7 at 9:00am. (we have 45 minutes)

Dan, I'd like you to brief Bruce and me on how the ELL training transition from in-person to on-line or web based is progressing, problems that you've encountered, and your plan for ELL in the coming years. As you know, one of our requests over a year ago was to begin moving the ELL training curriculum from in person to on-line. The premise was that in order to scale to meet the demand for MTT training that we envisioned, in-person training would become impractical due to the number of trainers that would be required, the time requirements for course implementation, and the rising cost of maintaining these programs.

If this premise is incorrect, please show us why. We need to know what you have done over the last 18 months to either test or actually move components of the ELL program to an on-line format. It would be helpful if you presented examples of where you are seeing success using on-line training, and where we are having problems.

How has your current plan been crafted to align with our Mission and Vision?

As you know, one of my performance indicators for FY14 is to see the number of on-site ELL events reduced from what is currently planned (over 50) to something leaner (8 has been suggested). We need to find out from you if this target is appropriate. If not, we need to know/understand why not. You did a good job of introducing me to the rationale for your current plan. Now I'm asking you to make your case before the CEO.

Thanks!

Brent

CHAPTER THREE
Christmas In Nepal

"If I paint a wild horse, you might not see the horse... but surely you will see the wildness!"

— **Pablo Picasso**

Keyword: Vision

Webster 1828: 1. The act of seeing external objects, actual sight. Faith here is turned into vision there. 2. Something imagined to be seen, though not real. 3. In Scripture, a revelation from God, an appearance or exhibition of something supernaturally presented to the minds of the prophets, by which they were informed of future events.

Google 2020: The faculty or state of being able to see. The ability to think about or plan the future with imagination or wisdom.

Noted Changes:

- Action vs faculty
- Expression of faith removed

- Wisdom added vs example of revelation from God

Location: Bonita Springs, Florida, October 2014 and Nepal, December 2014

There's something special about the heat of a bonfire in the cold at night. At the foothills of the Himalaya Mountains, where my bedroom was 50 degrees during the day, the bonfire became a quick friend. One night was special because translators gathered together after a two-week workshop where they translated most of the four gospels. Never before was the language group able to hear the Christmas story in their own language. We thought it would be a great event to celebrate Christmas a little early, teach the group about s'mores, sing some worship songs, and read from each of the gospels. Just about every range of emotion ran through the group that night, but the western guests who helped to facilitate the event were probably the quietest around the fire, and not just because of the difference in language. For me, I was in awe that I got to be there and witness God's testimony through sending His son to us. I could see the joy and the reverence in people because they were hearing the story for the first time. It was a true celebration moment for me after a lot of effort to have MAST fully understood by leadership within Wycliffe Associates.

Not everyone understands what is created out of the mind of an individual. Having lived, breathed, prayed, and thought about MAST for nearly a year before that event in Nepal, MAST seemed like a no-brainer in my mind. In that sense, I was not only naïve to the reality of how MAST was seen in the world of Bible Translation,

23

I was naïve to the reality of how it was perceived within my own organization.

For years, I have had the privilege of attending one of our organization's banquets, which was called "The President's Summit." It focused on the many who were highly financially committed to the cause. It was a weekend event and was an outpouring of how God used Wycliffe Associates to advance Bible translation. The outpouring was largely given by Bruce, who shared specific reports about the global scope of activity, as well as the vision of where we were to go as an organization. At the event in October 2014, I listened to Bruce's presentation. He got to a slide that had information about our pilot project on it. He gave some information about what the program was, but he quickly admitted he didn't quite know what the program was or what its potential was for our organization.

At that time, MAST caused quite a bit of confusion in regard to where it fit in. The pilot project had successfully engaged four experienced Bible translation teams of different languages and taught them the methodology. Our goal was to take ten-year New Testament projects and translate a sample of Scripture to see if we could reduce the timelines for translation and maintain the quality. The test, in short, was to see if we could increase the pace so much that, if successful, it would lead to forty-week New Testament completions using small translation teams. We had achieved success in all four groups, which was quickly relayed in messages back home. Bruce, promptly put out some Facebook messages that, to his surprise, caused quite a response. I thanked him later for being the one to look like a crazy person talking about impossible goals instead of me. After the pilot project, no one really knew what to do with MAST. They didn't know what it meant or where it fit within the structure of what our organization needed to pursue. On top of that, Bruce found out that there were many people ready and willing to take up the role of critic to knock down what we were trying to do.

In the conference, when Bruce talked about MAST from the stage and admitted he wasn't exactly sure of what MAST was or what it was going to do for translation, he expressed, "I have to go see it."

I smiled to myself. "Game on!"

At the pilot project, a fifth language group interrupted the event and also asked for Scripture, but the group was different from others. The group was not trained and did not receive our pre-MAST training. Yet, two young men walked out of the mountains, after hiking for two days, to get to Kathmandu and ask us to help them translate Scripture. Prior to their interruption of our event, I oversaw the facilitation of four teams that would complete the translations. So, I found myself extremely nervous to try the methodology I pushed for. Regardless of my nerves, there was no way we could send two men anywhere except to a table to begin translation. After four hours, they had their first chapter of Scripture translated and I witnessed the younger man, in his teens, cry at the sound of those words. Two things happened that day. First, I wondered how many teens in my culture cry for Scripture? Second, I prayed right there to see as many people as possible experience the same thing.

The two men went home and we gathered others in an attempt to translate the entire New Testament in two weeks. Unfortunately, we hoped for twenty-six people to do it, but only thirteen were able to come. Despite the lower number, our measurements were correct and in those two weeks, we translated and checked half of the New Testament. That was the event Bruce had to see, and I am thankful he did.

A couple days before the bonfire, I found myself sitting outside with some executives. Bruce, Brent, Tim Neu, the Vice President of Finance (now our COO), and Deborah Mullins, the Vice President of Training and Recruiting, put me in a circle to have a conversation about MAST. At least there was no fire in that circle.

"We understand the potential of this program and also the need to elevate you and the program within the organization. What do you need to make this work?" Bruce asked.

At that moment, I am sure I had a variety of expressions dancing in my head from comical to strategic to a whole bunch of selfish wish list items. I collected my thoughts and asked for two things. "I need full program control and a lot of money to facilitate it," I responded. I could have asked for anything at that time. There were conversations about position, authority, where to place the program, preferences, and wishes. However, I only wanted what I believed God put in our hands to be used and used fast. Bruce responded with incredible support that he has continued to live up to, as have all the VPs at Wycliffe Associates.

What I expressed in that moment was not want, control, desire, or wishes. It was vision. What I hadn't realized was that until the moment when Bruce and other leaders could see and touch MAST, they wouldn't see the potential I tried to communicate. While I tried to paint a wild horse, they were not seeing the horse at all—only the wildness of the idea. Once the program was seen, everything changed and Bruce followed with, "Now, later this week, you need to show me how this can work and scale up around the globe." The bonfire celebration was short lived, but believe me, it was a multi-level celebration for me.

The next morning, shortly after tea time, Bruce followed up on his statement about scaling up the program. We sat at a table and I pulled out a scrap sheet of paper and began listing partner organizations we had served by teaching English. I told him that since June, we had already started two languages in China. We believed we had several languages in India among seven partner organizations (as the meeting was scheduled after the event) and we were talking about more in China and Southeast Asia. In all, I listed a potential of seventy languages over the next year. That was enough to step forward.

The following January, Wycliffe Associates shut down for a half-day meeting to communicate the organizational turn we were going to make to scale MAST. Bible translation was not the only piece that would accelerate; everyone in the organization would feel it in their own lives, but at the time we had no idea what we were in for.

BIBLICAL FOUNDATION: A BURNING BUSH, NUMBERS 20, AND THE JOURNEY OF MOSES

Vision comes from God.

Moses was given something—God in a burning bush—that I am pretty sure none of us have ever received. From that moment on, Moses received vision with no hope of turning back. Throughout his life, Moses was given many leadership tasks within his mission. Moses, knowing the vision within the mission, continued to lead a group of people that often grumbled. At certain moments, that grumbling height-ened frustration, and Moses harshly reacted, sometimes even in disobedience to God. This can be the tension between vision (what is seen) and trying to express it to others. One of those frustrating moments for Moses was when he struck a rock for water. While it appeased the grumbling people by providing water, it took away the glimpse of God they really needed to see.

The reality is, vision is a burden. It's a burden of responsibility to express what God has given a person and to share it with others that were not given the same view of that picture. Moses was given many things to share among his people, including the plagues that were coming, how to prepare for Passover, how to leave Egypt, how to wander through the desert, the Ten Commandments, the tabernacle, etc. All of these were visions of what God had for his chosen people, yet he somehow found himself in a very human moment of disgruntled behavior and he expressed frustration. Imagine if Moses did that all the time as he portrayed a picture of vision that was only from his skills, and the people who followed him were only able to see his human side and not what God had given him. That would mean utter failure for the Israelites.

Unfortunately, much of today's expression of vision, has become humanized and the central focus is on peo-ples' skills not God's provision. Today, vision is killed by jealousy. Many believe vision is attached to role, authority, notoriety, expertise, or position. That is the worldly definition of vision. Even when it is acknowl-edged that vision comes from God and people react to it from a worldly point of view, the vision becomes endan-gered. That is why Moses continued to move through course corrections when he diminished what God did.

In contrast, when vision is acknowledged as coming from God, and it is expressed through His terms and through the people He chooses, we experience a different situation. We get elevation of what God wants to happen, acknowledgement of the appropriate task, advancement for involvement and accomplishment of goals, and unity in the Spirit. That is the story of the how God brought MAST into the vision within Wycliffe Associates. Leadership showed patience in the midst of frustration. They reflected on how to identify what God was doing, how the message was carried and how to best react to the situation. This is not a seeking of a praise moment for Wycliffe Associates, it is a reflective moment for how to evaluate vision and what it takes to be open to His movement and call.

MAST METHODOLOGY

Today, through MAST, the church is rising with the ability to express vision. God is raising up leaders like the two Nepali men I mentioned previously to bring those He calls to the forefront to say, "Yes you do need Scripture and you can do this." it is then our call to offer up the tools and resources we have so we can express, through love, how to be part of that vision.

God is not compartmentalized. This task of Bible translation is expressed through Mathew 14, Mathew 28 and Revelation 7 as a determined and destined timeline. We can choose to see vision as "a person who steps forward to lead" because he has a look into something in the future as an outcome or we can choose to say, "God has an assignment; it is His Word and we are responsive to that vision He has already purposed." This is weaving together around the world. Men and women responsive to the vision of God for His Word to go forth.

Whether you are called to support Bible translation in facilitation, translation, development, finances, or other ways, understand that it is a call to that vision. As you are called, the question, "Who am I?" is normal. Beyond that question is, "What is the vision God will call me to? How will I respond?" As well as, "What are my human potentials that could detract from acknowledging that this is of God, not man?"

ANALYSIS OF KEY WORDS

The largest change in the definitions above is a shift from revelation of God to the thought of wisdom with no mention of God. In expressing vision in this way, it is as if we are doing the same as Moses did—striking the rock in our own will and painting the picture for others that it is our power, not God's.

A LOOK AT KEY(ED) WORDS

An email from Deborah Mullins, Vice President of Recruiting and Training for Wycliffe Associates, sharing one of Bruce's initial reactions to MAST on Facebook in late June 2014.

Dan,

I had a chance to skype with Bruce yesterday about MAST. One of the things I mentioned was the possibility of me coming back to Nepal in Nov/Dec to help test your new model. It is looking very promising that I will be able to return (if you would still like me on the team). He was quite excited about the new model you are hoping to test. This morning I logged on to Facebook and saw this post:

 Bruce Smith
1 hr ·

How many local Christians would it take working as a team to draft an entire New Testament in their language in just 30 days?

Like · Comment · Share

I think he's just a little excited about your test idea.

Blessings,

Deborah

CHAPTER FOUR

There is a Madness to the Method

"Don't always complain the way isn't there. If you can't find the way, create it."
— **Israelmore Ayivor**, *Leaders' Frontpage: Leadership Insights from 21 Martin Luther King Jr. Thoughts*

Key Word: Method

Webster 1828: A suitable and convenient arrangement of things, proceedings or ideas; the natural or regular disposition of separate things or parts; convenient order for transacting business, or for comprehending any complicated subject.

Google 2020: 1. a particular form of procedure for accomplishing or approaching something, especially a systematic or established one.
2. orderliness of thought or behavior; systematic planning or action.

Noted Changes:
- Complicated subject
- Convenient order

Location: Bamenda, Cameroon, February 2015

"Why do you hate training?" A man asked at the first MAST event held in Africa.

"I don't hate training. I'm a teacher," I replied to him in a room of thirty trained Bible translators. "I think some training is backward and we have to measure it in effectiveness."

My response didn't appease some men and women who had their arms folded and eyebrows furled. Little did I know at the time, it didn't even appease my interpreter standing next to me who was also skeptical that MAST could work better than what they were using for Bible translation.

The large group of thirty had split up into their language groups. They were translation teams of six to ten translators. An hour later, I made it a point to visit the man who asked the question and observe his reaction to the methodology. He sat quietly. Soon, he took out some paper, glanced at a Bible (which was the one he had translated before he became a leader), and I watched him trying the steps of MAST. Later, the same man testified, "My New Testament needs a revision." That statement followed with his testimony affirming the MAST process and how the translations being produced in this initial workshop in Cameroon were better than those that they had been doing over the last years and decades of their work. Others stood and expressed similar testimonies each day of the event, which turned a room of serious skeptics into joyful believers in the process.

What caused the change so quickly? Yes, it is a work of God. Yes, it is the breath of the Holy Spirit, but it is

33

also the use of good teaching methodology. So what is this methodology?

MOBILIZED ASSISTANCE SUPPORTING TRANSLATION (MAST)

Step 1—Consume: Read (or listen) for understanding. (5–7 minutes)

> Each person will privately read, in the source text, his/her assigned Scripture passage striving to understand both the meaning and main points of the passage.

Step 2—Verbalize: In the target language, share with one other person, the Scripture passage that you have read. Include the following information: (2–4 minutes)

> 1. Tell the other person what you read; what are the big idea(s) in this passage?
> 2. What are the important things and details that you read?
> 3. What are the main events and people; what did they do?
> 4. What are the key concepts or key words in this passage?

Step 3—Chunk: Mark the chunks in your Scripture passage.

Re-read the passage of Scripture and divide it into manageable parts—or chunks—usually 1–4 verses. Each chunk should be the largest complete thoughts that you can remember and quickly rewrite. Mark them in your source text.

Step 4—Blind Draft: Each translator reads one chunk; close your source text (flips the paper over) and, skipping a space between lines, quickly write that chunk in your mother-tongue. Read and blind draft each chunk, one at a time, until all the chunks of your Scripture passage are written. Type text into a computer whenever possible. The goal is to express the meaning in natural language. Do not expect this draft to be perfect. Remember, this is your first draft; it will be refined.

Step 5—Self Edit: Open the Scripture passage and compare what you have written to the source text. Make Appropriate corrections. Make sure that all of the key elements are included, no text is added or omitted, and the meaning of the source text is clearly translated. Check details and key words. (Mark keywords in the source text.)

Step 6—Peer Edit: Switch papers and have another member of your team edit what you wrote. Ask questions and make suggestions of ways the writer can improve the translation. Make needed changes.

Read in comparison to the source text. You are not looking for word for word or even verse by verse translation, you are looking to make sure the

Author's Intended Meaning (AIM) of the passage is communicated.

Is anything missing? Is it natural? Does it sound good in your language? Is it smooth? Is it pleasing to your ear? Is it clear and understandable? Is it accurate? Are all the details there? Is the meaning of each of the keywords clearly communicated? (Mark keywords in the source text.)

When everyone in your small group has completed peer editing the passage, begin checking steps 7 and 8. If others have not finished, you may begin translating your next passage starting with Step 1.

Step 7—Keyword Check: Your small group (or a different team member) will read the key words in your passage making sure they are clearly communicated in your translation. *Note: a **key word** is one that, if left out, would change the meaning of the text. A **key term** is one of important theology like: Father, Son of God, Holy Spirit, glory, sanctification, etc.*

- What key words were used in the source text? *Highlight, underline or circle them in the source text.*
- Was the original meaning of each keyword accurately communicated in the mother tongue translation?

Step 8—Verse-by-verse Check: One person in your group (**not** the one who translated) will read out loud the Scripture passage, verse by verse, while the others listen. One may mentally back translate, comparing to the source text. Others will ask: Does it sound good in your language? Is it clear?

Smooth? Is it natural? Is it pleasing to your ear? Is it clear and understandable? Is it accurate? Are all the events and important details from the source text present? Is the meaning of the source text and each of the keywords clearly communicated? Is anything missing?

Each member of you group may focus on one or two of the above questions and make suggestions for improving quality of the translated text. Other translations, resources, and translation helps are available for use in this step. **Make appropriate changes to the translated text.** If you are not satisfied, pray about it and ask God for guidance. Also, ask others for input. Some things may not be resolved at this time and may require further consultation to clarify.

Back at the Kitchen Table, 2013

The night before the meeting with Bruce, while MAST was conceptualized as a process, there was the question about church checking. I asked, "Why is the church checking the work six months later? And how would I feel as a student if I received feedback to my assignment after six months?" Those questions helped me see Bible translation through the eyes of a teacher versus the eyes of a linguist. As that evening continued, I asked other "teacher-type questions," which included:

- Why is the timeline for translation so long when I know I have seen students write at paces much faster?

- Why isn't the checking of the work done as fast as possible?
- Why is there so much front-loaded learning with the expectation that it is going to transfer into process?
- How are they using elements of ownership in error correction?
- How are they using resources to own writing process in translation?
- How are they using higher level thinking?
- What is being lost in the long-term ratios of interacting with language?
- How are peers being used in the process of editing?
- Why are there only a few translators on a Bible translation team?
- What can we do to reduce the interruption to the brain switching between languages?
- How do we capture context at the same time we make translation bite-sized?

This book is not an attempt to answer the above questions, but it references the underlying perspective analyzing a way in which we could do those things. This is where MAST methodology was born.

All good methods are supported by good theories. All truth is God's truth, is one of the first phrases I heard expressed by professors at Moody. Meaning, if it is true and it is good, God owns that despite the human messes we make. Likewise, in education theory, even though it has gone in a very humanistic direction, when there is truth, God owns its good and will use it for others to benefit from. There are many theories that I was groomed under in both undergraduate and graduate education university programs. While I was at one of the more conservative teaching colleges in my undergraduate years, and one of the more bland-research-based (not liberal/conservative leaning) graduate schools, the theories were from many backgrounds. What was always a fun challenge for me was to see them with a filter of "God made our brains, our mind and our language ability and let's measure the theories to that." This helped form some of the use of theory in creating MAST.

Beyond the eight steps in MAST, we have a list of theories and approaches that number over fifty. Of those, we highlight about a dozen of them for our global facilitation teams. After the pilot project in Nepal, there was a quick call for expressing MAST in theoretical terms. With time pressing and little breaks in schedule, on December of 2014, on Christmas Eve, I quickly wrote a brief theory paper expressing the differences of Bible translation using MAST methodology. For those of you who love theoretical reading, please see the document in Appendix A. The lesson, however, was the discovery that I, without knowing it, was creating a comparison between MAST and traditional Bible translation.

AN UNINTENDED COMPARISON

Ervais was my French translator in Cameroon as I was fending off the questions of skepticism. Through events, I got to know Ervais well and found out that he too, at first, was a skeptic of MAST. Later, Ervais facilitated MAST events for us in two other countries and helped convert many of the traditional translation groups to MAST. Through this relationship and many others, I began to learn how big of a difference there is in the methods. When asked to do something different for Nepal, little did I know it would turn into me doing something different for Cameroon, and China, and Myanmar, and India, and more.

The skepticism took two paths—one was of curiosity, while the other was debate. Regardless, I had to learn the nuances of difference so I could do my best to express what we were doing and at the same time try not to offend what had been done for decades prior to MAST. That was easier said than done. Regardless, here are some of the differences that emerged:

- Linguistic philosophy. In a meeting with another organization involved in Bible translation, I attempted to express the perspective of how linguistics is taught at the university level versus a pure linguistics study. One is focused on breaking down the grammatical nuances of language for analysis (traditional) and the other is highly focused on language for use and meaning (MAST).

- Training first compared to training within. Traditional Bible translation includes training elements that include requirements of theology, language study, translation theory, and technology. This is done in many forms, but after some combination of these elements the translation process can begin. This training usually takes years. Using MAST, translation begins and the translators and translation itself is assessed for gaps in need and then surrounded with the needed resources or teaching to supplement the individualized needs.

- Expertise oversight compared to ownership of pieces. Traditional Bible translation, in large part, adopted a process of using foreign experts outside the target language and they oversee the process and manage the surrounding logistics and the quality of the Bible translation. Often, it is in the form of resources—financial, logistical and people—that provide guidance to the translation process, including quality through foreign consultant checking. MAST methodology differs from the traditional process because it is believed that the best process of Bible translation is to have oversight by those who speak the language. Further, elements of quality are assessed by those who speak the language in combination with the leadership of the church. They are the ones who steward the translation.

- Small groups compared to unlimited size groups. When the surrounding circumstances in Bible translation require heavy amounts of academic training, administrative oversight, and large financial resources, the investment in the team of Bible translators remains small and consists of a few translators contributing to the process. In MAST, with the removal of front-loaded training, outsider oversight, and high financial costs, the church is able to mobilize an unlimited number of contributors for the translation process.

- Pace. Traditional Bible translation with a national Bible translator averages about five verses per day in a draft format. MAST Bible translation averages about thirty-one verses a day in a checked format. With a team of only a few translators under each of the methodologies, it is possible for a MAST New Testament translation to occur in less than one year while a traditional model of translation can take up to ten years.

- Price. Due to the above circumstances, we have seen the price of a New Testament using traditional translation drop from hundreds of thousands of dollars to under twenty thousand dollars.

BIBLICAL FOUNDATION: JOHN 1

Many schools and teacher training institutions attempt to focus teachers on the art of lesson plan design. While this isn't a bad thing, it is very limited in comparison to developing methodology. With good methods, you can create any number of lesson plans for a range of teaching situations.

Before any of Jesus' miracles were recorded and before all the disciples were even gathered, Jesus was around people in multiple levels of instruction. Imagine asking Jesus, "Do you have a lesson plan?" The question would be odd, at best, especially when Jesus encountered unknown crowds in unknown ways with unknown expectations at any given moment. However, we should ask, "Did Jesus have a method?"

In the gospel of John, we see various expressions of a teacher. Whether referred to as a Rabbi, or teacher, or eventually understood as the Messiah, what did it take to get people to that level of comprehension? What did Jesus do? He asked, "What are you seeking?" (1:38) and then he challenged by saying "Come and you will see" (1:39). From those two steps, whatever truly happened between those verses, we do not know, but

42

Andrew went from understanding Jesus as a teacher to introducing Him as Messiah.

This happened again a few verses later when Philip was called to go see and Jesus told Philip to follow Him. A few verses later, Philip expressed to Nathaniel that Jesus was the Messiah and challenged Nathaniel to go see Him. Method taught, method transferred. We will never know exactly what was said; however, the results yielded the necessary outcome.

Methodology is the simple, orderly, obtainable process that we see produces the biggest transformation possible. Often, however, in creating something on paper, it is the perfect plan humans desire to make that forget who we are engaging—people. As a methodology is created on paper, it is far from the complexity that plays out in a group of people. It is those people who need to see it.

MAST METHODOLOGY

"Come and see" is a phrase that relates to MAST in every sense of its growth. Whether in Cameroon where we had skeptics at the table, or the staff from our English program transitioning into a new role or another doubter who asks, "Can anything good for Bible translation come out of Wycliffe Associates?" Our answer is "Come and see." We do our best to let God do His work on those who open their hearts to truly see.

ANALYSIS OF KEY WORDS

The loss of expressing methodology as a way to teach "the comprehension of complicated subjects" is a big loss. Today, we live in a world where expertise is valued more than the challenge of giving things away to rise to the next challenge. This is not only a sense of selfishness, it is a sense of oppression. The strongest comment I heard about MAST in Cameroon was, "This methodology gives us our dignity back."

Prior to my trip to Cameroon, I was told that MAST could work in Asia but not with Africans. Whether it was the belief that Africans couldn't obtain complicated processes through simple methodology or something else, we needed to refuse the belief and rise to the challenge that God desired for us. We had to come to terms with the great mystery. We took what was incomprehensible in a Savior who came to us in human form and died for us, and we made those stories as simple and acceptable to consume as possible.

A LOOK AT KEY(ED) WORDS

An Email Chain Including Ervais, my translator in Cameroon
On Jun 1, 2016, at 6:28 AM, Ervais wrote:

Dear Dan,

I hope you are fine. I have a question for you. How do you normally deal with teams that do not have a writing system? Some of the teams of Gabon do not have one. What would you advise here? Thanks

Ervais

Dan's Reply:

Hi Ervais

First, congratulations on your baby. Pretty soon you will catch up to me. :)

Thanks for the email. I will probably ask you more questions than you asked me. For languages that have no writing we have only a couple of options: 1. Borrow the national language if it works. If this is acceptable to the people group we can use it. If not, it is for taking the text from written form to oral and the recording is what becomes the product. 2. Do they have a phonetic match that is common (usual no) and then the same question—would the church and community accept it? 3. We move it to an all oral project which we have been doing better and better because we've developed a tool for tablets called translation recorder. I can bring tablets with this. It's worked very well in India and China (almost to pace of one chapter a day).

The bigger question is literacy—can these translators read source text?

This leads me to some questions:

1. Do you know how many languages for sure and how many per group?

2. For the written projects what equipment is needed? Is CABTAL bringing or is WA? Paratext or translation studio?

3. For oral projects, if you have numbers, I can bring tablets for recording. At a minimum two per language team (more is better).

I'll stop there and I realize you may not have some of the answers.

Glad you are going, but hope your life and schedule is ok! I am bringing Leah (for French) our Vice President and two men from DRC that I want to groom into MAST. (They have a very large church network.)

Please keep asking questions for how I can support.

Dan

CHAPTER FIVE
Throwing Money Out the Window

"Anything that just costs money is cheap."
— **John Steinbeck**

Key Word: Value

Webster 1828: Worth; that property or those properties of a thing which render it useful or estimable; or the degree of that property or of such properties.

Google 2020: the regard that something is held to deserve; the importance, worth, or usefulness of something

Noted Differences:
- Worth changed to regard in the beginning— worth is not synonymous, but a character- istic within
  - Webster 1828, the word worth is synony- mous with value
  - Google 2020, worth is defined as equivalent in value to the sum or item specified
  - Google 2020, regard is to consider or think of (someone or something) in a specified way

Location: Between Jos and Abuja, Nigeria 2018

I remember my mom talked about heating bills when I was a child. She used the phrase, "Throwing money out the window." After driving down a road in Nigeria, however, I'll never think of that phrase the same. Instead, that phrase will forever remind me of Cyrill, my driver. For those who are involved in travel on the roads in Nigeria understand that your driver is very important. The driver makes all the difference in the world—not for time or payment, but for safety.

Cyrill was a fifty-one-year-old man who looked about thirty-five. He drove a route from Abuja to Jos several times a week. The road was filled with stories of kidnappings, car thefts, robberies, and senseless shootings. When I spoke to him about a map and routes, he happily showed his strategies. Even prepared with all the information though, I don't recommend it. It will only stress you out more. He told me about all the bad things that happened and I could see places on the map that I could not avoid.

All that said, between the military and police check points (about twenty on a five hour drive) you can see some good things, too. You can see Cyrill's relationship with almost every check point person along the road. When conflict arises, he shares, "These are missionaries," so that people seeking a bribe turn away. Cyrill will toss a few dollars out the window from time to time, too. Sometimes it goes to those who take it upon themselves to patch the road. This helps avoid slowdowns in the most dangerous places. One time, he gave money to a legless man who sat on the road begging. The beggar wheeled over on his makeshift wooden imitation of a skateboard to grab the wrinkled currency, then waved a *thank you* and went back to his position.

Cyrill was a Christian who understood our mission. He understood what his nation needed. His country has nearly two hundred million people and they speak more than three hundred languages. Nearly two hundred and thirty of those languages still need a Bible translation.

Nigeria is one of the top three countries with Bible translation needs. Our hope is to build a plan to start on the languages that are left in the next three years. Despite persecution, dangers, limited funding, changes in direction, and economic challenges that don't see any hope of change in the next several years, we understand what is at stake. Further, we have a passion to fight the battle and win.

My question to us is, do we value people like Cyrill enough to throw money out the window to pave a way for change?

Location: Aurangabad, India, 2018

What if all you knew about your identity was a gesture. Imagine going to bed each night questioning who you are because you don't have a name.

I met an eighteen-year-old girl in India who was brought to us at a teaching event. She was found by a loving, deaf community in India. We held a teaching event for people who were deaf and illiterate and had never been in school. The girl did not have a name. She was deemed unworthy of one because she wouldn't be talked about or taken to events or any type of social gatherings. Once discovered, deaf people who were involved in Bible translation wanted to do something for her. They wanted to give her a name. Collectively, about a dozen people showed her how they select names for one another. Basically, they look at the person, determine some characteristics, then give a few name suggestions. In the end, the girl chose a gesture of a swipe of her hand just above her forehead and then over her hair.

Unfortunately, that is the story for over seventy percent of deaf people around the world. They are isolated, have a few gestures for basic functioning, and are often given up on by others. That was a small part of the story that week. The leaders who helped name her were people I met eighteen months earlier. They were deaf people who knew sign language. When I met them, they were timid, afraid, and some of them were beaten for showing up to our event. They learned to be deaf Bible translators. On April 22, 2018 they celebrated with one hundred fifty people (ninety percent were non-Christian) because they finished the second deaf video of the New Testament in the world in less than eighteen months. The video translation of the Bible used Marathi Sign Language. The first translation in American Sign Language took more than thirty years.

It was a historic event accomplished by people who had supernaturally grown in maturity. The team was no longer timid. They were Christian leaders who took in a new group of students and taught them that they could understand Scripture even if they didn't know sign language.

Let me explain the room I spent several days in. There were deaf leaders who completed their Bible. The video Bible would serve four hundred thousand deaf Marathi speakers. Leaders in the room learned to teach something new. A handful of people called "home sign" deaf people were also in the room. Like the girl mentioned above, they were non-Christians who came to see if they could learn something. There's no literacy. There's no sign language. There's only the hope that the use of the new system could teach them a way to communicate.

After four days, we saw each of the home sign deaf people were able to read Scripture through symbols. When friendships bloom. We saw wide-eyed staring become vibrant participation. We saw serious faces learn what a natural smile of joy feels like. Most importantly, we saw that most of the forgotten people could understand Scripture. But there were others in the room.

Two boys who were considered deaf and blind were among the participants. Each boy had a relative with them. One of the boys was fifteen years old and was with his mom. The other boy was eighteen years old and with his grandpa. Both boys lived in a home and they received basic care. The fifteen-year-old was able to see things within an inch of his face. It was a special challenge to see if we could teach them about God's Word. For the two boys, we used symbols on 3D printed cards that they could touch and learn from. Using props and tapping for "yes" and "no," it took four days to teach them a dozen words.

By the fourth day, we were able to help the eighteen-year-old understand a fragment of a passage. It doesn't seem like much, but considering he lived eighteen years with very few words in his vocabulary, we were pleased with the progress. The fifteen-year-old was able to conceptualize and produce sentences.

Over a few days, we noticed that while he was only able to see an inch in front of him, we saw him react to things around the table—a few feet away. Not knowing the full story, we surmised that not only had others given up on him, he had probably given up too and was resolved to keep his head down.

There's a lot left to do. All three groups—Sign language, home sign and deaf-blind—have large, unreached populations. In India alone, there are three more sign languages in translation and eleven more that need to start. Once those groups are engaged, the other audiences—deaf-no sign language and deaf-blind—will follow.

I can't begin to tell you the full story or the range of challenges, but I can tell you I met some amazing Christians that week in India. They are giants of the faith that no one will ever know in this world. However, when you arrive in heaven, I want you to find the people who are there who went years without a name because they will be there, too.

To begin to even comprehend this, the question, "Do we value these people?" needs to be asked. What is their worth? Do we believe they matter? If so, where are the deaf and the deaf illiterate with no sign language, and the deaf blind, in our churches? They exist in every culture and country, and the numbers in those populations are large.

Location: Michigan, 2002

When I heard that a student's father had been shot in a Detroit-area church, I was in shock. As the weeks went on, I wondered, "Is anyone doing anything to help the student?" Rumors swirled about why the shooting had happened, but it was evident that no one knew what to do to help the student. Much the same, I didn't know what to do to, but because he was a second language learner, I had an inroad to intervene on his behalf.

There were rumors that this student was pressured by his family to avenge his father's death by killing someone from the family that killed his father. That was the root cause of why the student's father was killed in the first place. The repetitious killing dated back to the country they had immigrated from. Imagine the perplexing and challenging classroom dynamic to even attempt to course correct the student toward his education. Instruction, homework, and graded assignments were not going to help. The only thing I could do is get to some level of understanding about why the shooting occurred and show the student that he had value. Between lessons, I was able to get to know the family and even take the student to my college courses in the evenings. I hoped he would see potential in his future.

Sometime after trying to help the student, I had the opportunity to go to the country his family immigrated from. I visited a school district that was closest to the region they came from, and I befriended the psychologist for the entire school district. We sat together one evening drinking coffee, the power flickered in and out on us and he explained to me that the problem was not a phycological one. He told me about a book that was written several generations ago. The book contained rules, laws, and codes to live by. During different times of occupation, people fled to the mountains to take refuge and the book was used to keep order in society. Various requirements, which included revenge killing for certain things, were laid out in the book. The information was particularly shocking until I asked, "Where did this book come from?" The psychologist said, "The priests." For years, I didn't understand that it was a problem of Bible translation and the lack of Scripture in desperate communities. That's one part of this story.

52

The other part of the story is how to help a non-Christian person, who lost his father, find his self-worth and walk away from his expected path of revenge.

THE QUESTION OF VALUE

Whether I was teaching middle school students, training teachers, preparing teams to teach English at Wycliffe Associates, or preparing teams to facilitate MAST, I always said, "If we understand individuals and we value them, we have the opportunity to be successful." From there, I generally teach five value traits for facilitation. These traits include finding common interest (between student and teacher), honesty, praise, protection, and service. These traits are particularly powerful tools when it comes to childrearing, teaching, and work. I have also found them to be powerful aids helping people discover their self-worth.

Imagine the beggar with no legs—from the beginning of this chapter—who just received a small amount of cash tossed from a car window. The value of that money extends beyond the money itself because not only is money in short supply in Nigeria, but also because a person who would throw it out the window is even more rare.

Think about the nameless girl who had never had anyone communicate with her in a meaningful way and how she found friends who cared enough to think about her and find a name that expressed who she was.

Take the student who lost his sense of family security and was trained in a belief system the stemmed from a long line of religious men. He found someone who would take the time to understand why his life experiences happened and be able to tell him that he had value beyond his perceived destiny.

The power of MAST is more than a method. It's more than a bunch of theories. It is a command of two forms — the Great Commission and showing love to one another. The urgency motivating MAST is more than an urgency to get Scripture out into the world. It is valuable to people who are dying without it. Do we value all audiences enough? If so, what does that value look like? Is it urgent? Is it relative to need or provision, or does it transcend what we have?

Biblical Foundation

- **Please read:**
  - ○ **Matthew 28:16-20**
  - ○ **John 13:34-35**
  - ○ **Matthew 22:38**

Think about the examples where Jesus stopped to take the time to express value to others. Some of them through healing and others through teaching. As the later chapters of the gospel continued, the expression of mission and love emerged. While many themes fit throughout Scripture, love is undeniable and the value of that love has action to it. It does for us as well. As Jesus commissioned us to go, he also told the disciples that they were to be known by their love. Loving one another is about the inherent value and worth in others. While part of me feels there is nothing new in this thinking, another part of me is astounded how easy it is for us to miss things. It is shocking how a little bit of energy put forth in expressions of value impact others. From this, I find the real challenge is being open and listening to what God calls us to do.

ANALYSIS OF KEY WORDS

The change in this definition is a little harder to grasp because the words "value" and "worth" cross over so much in meaning. At one point, they were synonymous, today "worth" is within the definition, so it needs more context. For example, if you were to use the 1828 definition of "value" and "worth" for pizza you would say that pizza has value and worth as a whole entity. However, when we separate out "worth, we would say pizza has value, but it's worth is (and place a marker on it of some qualifier).

This is great for functional language, but when you place people into the middle of that definition, it changes quite a bit. Using the same example as above, imagine saying, "People have value, but their worth is _____." Words that were once synonymous are now separate at times and they impact our logic and thinking more than we know. You may argue that you still see them synonymously, but society does not. There is a qualifier on the worth of human life today that did not exist in 1828 when we see the issues of abortion and euthanasia as tolerated behaviors. This same definition of "worth" plays out in multiple ways, including those who have disabilities, those who are considered untouchable or unfixable, and even those we simply don't see.

A LOOK AT KEY(ED) WORDS

A Sample of Curriculum Outline for How to Train Facilitators in MAST:

Values—teach these traits as "these are characteristics of how to value people:

Share each of the categories in the form of a picture—have the students draw a picture and you explain the traits and why they are important.

Value in 5 Traits:

1. Honesty (picture of a tree) —Honest assessment
   Constructive reinforcement
   Careful with words

2. Common Interest (picture of a triangle)—Find the common ground
   Harder to leave a person than a project.
   Spend time with each other
   Round-table discussions/collaboration

3. Praise (Write the word WOW!)—Give compliments—truthful ones
   Show personal care.
   Specific complements are more meaningful
   Treat each person individually

4. Protection (picture is a shield)—
   Acknowledge support
   Never quit improving
   Listen to the fears of others
   Keep others' needs in mind

5. Serving others (picture of a smiley face with a heart)—Do work for someone else
   Looking out for others' needs
   Offering to fill in the gaps

Express the following points:
- Without value, motivation drops over time.
- With value, you can motivate, but also correct and redirect.
- The issue of quality and value go together—if you can correct, you can improve. If you can protect, people are more willing to make mistakes and use natural language.

CHAPTER SIX

Does God Have Favorites?

"This is what the past is for! Every experience God gives us, every person He puts in our lives is the perfect preparation for the future that only He can see."
— **Corrie Ten Boom,** *The Hiding Place*

Key Word: Faith

Webster 1828: Belief; the assent of the mind to the truth of what is declared by another, resting on his authority and veracity, without other evidence; the judgment that what another states or testifies is the truth.

Google 2020: complete trust or confidence in someone or something

Noted Difference:
- Absence of truth
- Sense of authority vs trust in someone/something

Location: Orlando, Florida

66 **I**f you figure about a hundred translators are gathered, I think we could see a whole Bible done in a two-week period of time," Robert expressed, being more brave than most as he sat across my desk in the Orlando offices. I'm sure some of the MAST team members had thought about this, but so far, no one had suggested it. There was a group in Southeast Asia that Robert believed was ready to take on the task of taking MAST to the next level. Ironically that familiar "Who am I?" question changed from the question of "Can we do this?" to "Who am I to stand in the way of what God can do?" That was the prompting I felt in my office, which was then followed by giving Robert the green light to make his attempt at the first whole Bible project.

Robert was brought to me at the request of Brent Ropp. Brent asked me if there was a potential role for Robert. Recently, Robert's wife had passed away, pulling him out of their assignment in the Pacific region. Not broken, but certainly searching, I had a meeting with Robert when I just started to build a staff for the English program. Robert was a couple of decades older than me and one of the first staff members to have life experience beyond my own. I found it humbling to be his leader. Robert was a practical man who was logical and honest. Robert didn't waste time beating around the bush debating if he could accomplish something. That worked well for me because having a staff member I could always use as a metric to express truth in programs with some quick and clear feedback was invaluable.

When Robert came to me with the suggestion of a two-week Bible translation, I knew he wasn't dreaming.

He was planning. I had to admit, I admired his faith—not just because of the God-sized event, but because Robert was a man who had lived a full life with all the ups and downs. He was ready to continue doing great things with God. Some people would retire in a situation like Robert's, and others would recover from the wounds of life, but Robert never let those types of thoughts enter his mind.

Robert is one example of many people on a staff that God built to facilitate MAST. Using Robert's lessons from past experiences, God blessed Robert in his faith. From that, we have seen some amazing firsts at Wycliffe Associates. Robert was the first facilitator to use MAST to see a complete a New Testament translation finish in a two-week workshop. Robert was the first person to attempt a whole Bible translation in two weeks. Robert was the first to see an Old Testament completion using MAST. Robert was the leader of the largest translation event known to date. It had more than five hundred participants who spoke ten different languages, and they worked on ten New Testament translations at the same time. We joked with Robert that he must have been God's favorite because he kept experiencing great accomplishments before anyone else. The truth is, Robert exercised big faith in a big God.

MIND THE GAP

If you've ever traveled to London and rode on the underground, you know the announcement "Mind the gap" that warns you to watch your step as you enter and exit the train cars. Most people can hear the phrase, but at the same time, ignore it.

Early in MAST, and sometimes even now, people wanted to know what made MAST work or what the theories were behind the program. I love these questions. At times, however, I just wanted to say, "God makes it work." People didn't want that answer, and there are plenty of theories behind the method, but I also wanted to say "Mind the gap." I never want MAST to become an effort of human endeavor. The method is not the recipe for success, it is the template for human interaction to take place. The recipe for success is to have the Holy Spirit in the room and the faith that God called us all to a big task that we can accomplish in spite of impossible odds.

When Wycliffe Associates facilitated ESL programs, we saw results far beyond the research curve. I know this because my previous life existed within the middle school classroom and I also trained future teachers in the college of education.

The normal growth for a second language student who doesn't speak English takes five to seven years to achieve academic fluency. If you divide up listening, speaking, reading and writing skill on a five-year scale, you realize it takes years to achieve each skill and demonstrate it at a fluent level. Documented in testing, writing samples and videos, we witness new language students achieve six to twelve months of education in a span of two and three weeks. Some participants referred to the program as a "miracle of language."

People would ask, "What's the secret?" While the team could point to theories they were trained in, there was still a gap of knowledge when it came to the explanation. We firmly believed our programs had good theory, good facilitation, and that it honored God. Through our faith, though, we got to see unprecedented growth. Our purposeful, integrated team devotions, student devotions, Bible teaching rotations, prayer rotations, and worship times were God honoring and we believe they demonstrated our communal leap of faith. Beyond the theories, we believe that in MAST there is a gap in all of our efforts and all our gained experiences that must be met with faith that God would do His work in the midst of the programs. That is the true backbone of what we do.

The opposite of this is us depending on our statistics, theories, and human wisdom, as well as believing that measurements would make the program successful. One morning at a workshop, a Bible translation consultant came to me with documents filled with statistics about the pace of translation in for-profit businesses to show me how impossible it was to attempt the pace we hoped to achieve with MAST. I smiled and politely refused to engage in a potentially lengthy discussion. I was asked, "Why I wouldn't consider this element of information and make some changes in expectations on outcomes." I replied, "Because I know, by faith, that we can reach the goals we were given." Today, this faith looks like a statistic for MAST at thirty-one verses per day, but at that time, it was a gap—a leap of faith that was setting a God-sized goal. One that was unprecedented in translation. Until now.

BIBLICAL FOUNDATION ELIJAH 1, KINGS 17 AND 18

What did it take for Elijah to stand before the prophets of Baal and be so amazingly bold? It took faith. While we could study, debate, and exegete over the exactness of what faith is, in a practical sense we can see that it was enough for Elijah to move forward in what God asked him to do. Elijah's existence in that faith was a combination of what was seen at the time and what was gained in prior experience. I used to love the story of Elijah standing there and sarcastically (in my mind) showing up the false prophets, I have since changed. The more I read about Elijah, the more I have grown fond of chapter 17 where a widow housed him. By obedience, Elijah went to the woman's home and, by faith, he called out to God to raise the widow's son from death.

Today, when I read chapter 18, I cannot help but remember the events prior that helped shape Elijah. What gave him that amazing, bold faith? His faith experiences before that did, and his obedience before that. Elijah could have chosen to do otherwise.

The faith of Elijah can live out in us today. Just as Robert could have retired, fled, or hid, he did not. He let his prior experiences and his ongoing obedience call him to more. From that, he received favor to be the one who got to see several special milestones in Bible translation. He wasn't the favorite, but he certainly found favor. Just as obedient translators enter what is often said to be impossible to have in a lifetime, in just days translators saw chapters emerge out of their efforts. We serve a big God.

MAST Methodology

MAST is based on well-researched theories. At times, it also requires leaps of faith. As the MAST movement started, it needed people to break the way of thinking that translation needed to take a decade or more. People also needed to break the routine of having to pay expert translators for their services. Furthermore, lead facilitators, like Robert, needed to take leaps of faith to see what was possible. There were some thoughts about pacing. There were some thoughts about theory and gathering. However, when you say, "If you gather a hundred people together and begin dividing up a whole Bible for translation within two weeks," you are not speaking from experience, logic, statistics, or logistics, you are speaking with faith alone. As we go deeper, the faith of people in persecuted areas, impoverished situations, and logistically challenging dynamics should not be dismissed.

No method, theory, or planning can replace the existence of faith. In fact, MAST is meant to create a gap so that we must depend on God in faith. Teams take the method and meet people for the first time. While we can try to project who and what skills are in the room, we would still be dealing with human diversity in individuals. There is no way to project what could happen at a MAST event. In the end, we have to rely on what God will do with the faithful. When people ask, "What do I need in the skills for MAST translators?" The answer is, "We need people with big faith."

ANALYSIS OF KEY WORDS

Of all the words to be considered important in this book, faith could be at the top of the list. It is no wonder that this word has been altered in English. Of all the words, this one has the most frightening alteration because the definition removes authority and shifts toward someone/something. Removing truth, which is the opposite of what Jesus came to testify to, is frightening and we would all be left to rely on our own set of systems and people. We should not do this. We should not blur out the reminders of what it is we need to remind ourselves of. This is more than "minding the gap", this is the essence of who we are in Christ.

A LOOK AT KEY(ED) WORDS

October 23, 2017 Robert Harmon responded to a leadership conversation, the topic "Die to One's Self"

This is something God has been teaching me for the past couple years–totally allowing God to have control of my life and live through me to bring honor and glory to Him.

I heard an excellent definition of commitment: "Giving all that I know of myself to all that I know of God." As I learn more about myself and/or more about God, that is a new area I need to commit to Him. It is an ongoing, never ending, process.

As I really trust Him and give Him total control of everything, it is a fantastic way to live–allowing Him to live IN and THROUGH me in all that I do!

CHAPTER SEVEN
Letting Go

"Sacrifice is a part of life. It's supposed to be. It's not something to regret. It's something to aspire to."
— **Mitch Albom**

Key Word: Sacrifice

Webster 1828: To offer to God in homage or worship, by killing and consuming, as victims on an altar; to immolate, either as an atonement for sin, or to procure favor, or to express thankfulness

Google 2020: an act of slaughtering an animal or person or surrendering a possession as an offering to God or to a divine or supernatural figure

Noted Differences:
- No mention of sin, favor or thankfulness

Location: Jos, Nigeria, October 2018

"I'm getting a phone call from home?" I said. It was from my wife, Holly, and I had a sense something was wrong because we typically texted. I had just settled into my familiar room at the translation campus in Jos. In a broken voice and words I don't quite remember, all I could make out was, "Dan, your mom died." I know there were other words that followed, but I can't remember them. I stared at the decorative design in the metal door of the room. I took a few minutes and everything hit me all at once. I thought about where I was, what we were doing, what needed to be done, and I thought about my dad.

Travel to Jos was not easy. It required a flight across the ocean to Europe, and then down to Abuja, Nigeria, which included an overnight stay, then a five to seven-hour drive that required leaving before dawn to avoid the bandits. Kidnapping and military, local police, and state police checkpoints were normal on the drive. I knew my arrival would immediately become a departure the next day. I invested a lot of time in Nigeria that year. That was my sixth trip in 2018 and we were supposed to launch two new programs, as well as a partnership with Our Daily Bread over the next two weeks. I had to hand the programs off to the team I had brought together so I could get home.

Within minutes of communicating my mother's passing, the partner organization's leadership gathered with me and the Wycliffe Associates team. They said, "In Nigeria, we have a saying that everything stops for death." We prayed, we sang, and we read Scripture. Just minutes before, I had been so upset that I was in Nigeria and so far away from my family, but in that special time of comfort, I realized God knew exactly where I needed to be.

It had only been three days since I last spoke to my mom. She wasn't feeling well, but continued to update me on her doctor's appointments and test results did not seem to point to any serious causes. She had another appointment the day before she died, and I had expected to get an update on that. I never expected to hear that my dad had found her on the floor in their bedroom. That image stuck in my mind the whole way home.

I prepared the team for what they would experience during the two weeks without me. By the end of our meeting, all I could do was pray and be at peace that God was in control. I had to let go of my responsibilities at the event. Ironically, this was not the first time this has happened. In 2011, as I landed in Cameroon, I received a similar text that my mother-in-law had passed away sooner than expected. At that time, I struggled to push the two leaders I had been grooming into the role of leadership before our next planned stops (Korea and Nepal).

Unfortunately, there are many layers involved in letting go. There is this reality of death, but there is also letting go of everything else as well. That includes our children, our possessions, our careers, our resources, our finances, etc. If I had not, I cannot imagine I would have been ready for that day in Nigeria, or so many others like it. Yet, there is a blessing behind letting things go.

On November 21, 2009, I was in my classroom in Michigan and enjoying my last year of teaching before moving into full-time ministry with Wycliffe Associates. I thought about what it would take to make the transition to my new position. We were in the worst economical time of our lives. The housing market took a downturn and I had just put in an offer on a home in Florida. I was on track to leave my job and its income behind, we had five children, and two homes and no idea how the situation would play out. By faith, I knew I had to go, but I was terrified. I sat at my desk, playing with numbers and income. I asked God, "How is this going to work?"

In frustration, but yet with peace, I closed my folder and said, "You know what God? You told me to go and I trust you, but please show me what I'm supposed to do."

I had parent-teacher conferences that evening. I sat in a meeting with a parent and I heard a whisper from God. "All of it," He said. I acknowledged the phrase but also ignored it, but the words wouldn't go away. "What does that mean? I am giving all of it." Yet, the words swirled in my head, still. Sometime later, I thought, "My teacher annuities." I thought I gave everything over, but I forgot I had stored some up. I was challenged with the thought of "Would you really give every bit of it up for me?" I was so relieved and so joyful inside that I'm sure even the student who thought they were coming for a bad parent conference felt relieved to see my smile. Suddenly, letting go became my gain in moving forward. However, that is not the end of the story.

My principal knew it was my last year of teaching, and he asked me into his office. He told me, "I got a call from Wycliffe Associates for a reference for you." I was comfortable in my relationship with my boss, so I shared some details. He said, "You're not going to believe this, but my father-in-law is the former president of Wycliffe Associates."

He was right, I couldn't believe it. We kept talking, and I jokingly said, "Hey, you're an administrator. In your district meetings, you need to tell them to buy out my contract so I can retire early." He laughed and affirmed the impossibility of my joke. That is, until one day, he came running into my classroom. "Do you know when things never happen and shouldn't happen, and are impossible, but they happen anyway?" He asked. I smiled and looked at him. "I got a buyout?" I asked. The amount of the buyout almost equaled the down payment for the home in Florida. That was the money I didn't have and why I asked God how it was all going to work. God asked me, "Will you give it all to me?" Letting go to God had a blessing behind it.

While the event in Nigeria had positive and negative outcomes, I was there four months later speaking with them about their organization's potential. We spoke about completing twenty-seven New Testaments in partnership with the church. I, however, encouraged one hundred or more translations over time. I said we would do it using a new methodology but it came with a lot of sacrifice in their relationships. The director of the organization said, "We like the vision, but under this model, how do we survive as an entity?" I loved the open discussion and I listed out everything they were doing. I then spoke about everything that needed to be done for Nigeria, including the two hundred languages that needed translations, as well as several hundred more that needed a complete Bible. In reality, if the organization could let go of what they had, they would create a larger and more fruitful role for Bible translation and Nigeria. The organization has since taken steps forward, but experience challenges, just as we all do when we let things go. Yet, there is a blessing to letting go.

In 2017, the department facilitating MAST grew, and I managed more than twenty people who were also in management roles. We restructured so we could have seven program leaders to take on portions of the department's management roles. As that happened, I no longer managed, facilitated, or was involved in MAST in the field. As I look back, if that had not happened, and if I had not let go, programs would not have been explored, people would not have received the time to join in because they were given personal attention and certain partnerships would not have existed. Today, apart from MAST, there is a whole new staff in a variety of programs. I don't believe we would have been able to spread programs out as far if I and many others had not let go. That's not to say I was the one who was critical in forming or doing those things, I mean that I wouldn't have had the opportunity to do them because I didn't let go of things.

BIBLICAL FOUNDATION LUKE 9

I never thought I would personally understand Jesus telling someone to follow Him and the denial of the request to first bury a parent. I now understand that passage as putting the importance of God in relationship to the importance of everything we have and when the time comes, will you let go of everything so He can give you what you don't see. When I told my mom about leaving for ministry, she did not take it well. My mom was a wonderful Christian, but she was also a mother who had six miscarriages and I was the youngest of her three children who survived. She didn't want to give me up. Over the years, she did it because she had to, but it was a harsh reminder that by following His call I was in Nigeria when she passed. Sacrifice is a reality in ministry, and as a Christian. That comes in many forms, and mine is not one to compare to those who give so much more sacrificially. Even so, the lesson should not be missed. We speak of a sovereign God. We speak of a God who cares about feeding birds. A Savior who pulled a coin from the mouth of a fish. A God who sacrificed His son and we can miss it still—sacrifice is part of our Christian heritage and that comes in many forms. With it is a blessing. Without it, what is there?

ANALYSIS OF KEY WORDS

Unfortunately, the phrase "letting go" is not in the dictionary, so "sacrifice" is one of the chosen words that relates. It is surprising to some to see the word hold the meaning that has biblical heritage to it. It is sad to see the loss of reflection of why that Biblical heritage gave us such terms. Society wants us to forget sin altogether. If sin doesn't exist in the words we use, then we don't have to reflect on it. If sin doesn't exist in our words of high action in refining ourselves, it will never happen. Sacrifice means we set aside our nature so we may have a new one. The loss isn't in the absence of the word or even the loss for us to be able to think about reflecting on sin. The loss is that we don't get to see the actions it takes to see the new we can have in a better way forward. In a renewed mind in Christ. Who wouldn't want to live in the joy of those traits?

A Look at Key(ed) Words

Wed Oct 10, 2018
Detroit Free Press   *All Zones*Detroit News   *All Zones*

Mary Lou Kramer

SOUTH ROCKWOOD - Mary Lou Kramer, age 80 of South Rockwood, passed away Saturday, October 6, 2018.

Born March 5, 1938 in Detroit, Mary Lou was the daughter of Stanley and Rozella (Zehnder) Spragg. She married the love of her life, Francis "Frank" Kramer on March 16, 1957 in Livonia.

A dedicated homemaker Mary Lou was a member of Charity Baptist Church. She enjoyed shopping and antiques.

Mary Lou leaves to cherish her memory, Frank, her husband of the past 61 years; children: Daniel (Holly) Kramer, David Kramer and Kenneth (Michele) Kramer; 9 grandchildren, 2 great grandchildren; as well as her siblings: Leatrice (Fred) Said and Marvin Spragg. Sadly she was preceded in death by her parents and 5 siblings.

Friends may call Thursday from 3pm until 9pm at the Ford Chapel-Martenson Family of Funeral Homes 23620 N. Huron River Dr., Rockwood. Funeral services celebrating her life will be Friday. She will lie in state from 10 am until the funeral service at 11am from Charity Baptist Church, 17380 Racho Rd, Brownstown. Burial to follow in Parkview Memorial Cemtery.

For more information, to leave an online condolence, or send a floral tribute, please visit www.martenson.com

CHAPTER EIGHT

Lifting Our Chairs in Worship

Opportunities multiply as they are seized
--Sun Tzu

Key Words: Multiply and Strategy

Webster 1828

Multiply: To increase in number; to make more by natural generation or production

Strategy No definition found

Google 2020

Multiply: increase or cause to increase greatly in number or quantity

Strategy: a plan of action or policy designed to achieve a major or overall aim

Noted Change:
- A new word that emerged in English just prior to 1828 that didn't make it into the dictionary

- Natural generation/production vs cause to increase

Location: Rukingiri, Uganda

"God, why did you bring me here?" I asked. I looked around at the humble facilities as some very nice, godly men showed me their ministry. Jet lagged and tired, I tried to focus on the message I was asked to deliver to a congregation of a few hundred people. I looked forward to the worship session because I hadn't heard the harmonized sound of central African singing in a long time. However, I couldn't help but think how the men and our surroundings were going to do what we had discussed in email. We talked about some big goals: building a training center, planting churches, discipling people through education platforms, and integrating Bible translation into the curriculum of that discipleship. Before arriving, my mind imagined classrooms, materials, and facilities that would help us meet those benchmarks. Not only did I not see anything I had imagined, but we were also in a very distant location within Uganda. I wondered how our remoteness would affect our service to such a tall task.

The thoughts in my head were interrupted when worship began. I did hear that familiar sound of harmonizing and witnessed a wonderful and energetic worship team. As time went on, I witnessed an increase in energy within the worship. It was joyful. It was loud. It was exciting, and it was wild! My eyes didn't know where to look: the stage, the pastors, or the congregation. Soon, they focused on the congregation as they waved scarfs and Bibles in the air. A few people who had neither to wave picked up their plastic chairs by one leg and held them high above their heads. The pastor checked to see if I was okay. He giggled and smiled as I smiled back, both of us knowing that experience was something I was not used to. I don't know the words to the song that day, but I do know everyone sung it in complete joy. I also know it is the one worship time I will never forget.

The next day, after some rest from my journey, we began a teaching session to explore how Bible translation could fit within the ministries of Rukingiri Community Church, which was part of Amiziba Ministries. I had a plan to teach ten leaders within the congregation, but I kept the plan loose so we could have more interaction.

At one point, a humble man, who I saw teach youth in Sunday School the day before, stood up and introduced himself. "My name is Paul, and I think we need to better share who we are with you. We haven't yet done that well." Paul spoke about the foundations and principles of ministry they lived by, which I read prior to the meeting. The difference was, Paul transparently spoke about them, then he focused on finances a bit.

He told me they made a budget for things and took tedious care of that budget by going line by line. At the end of an event, they sat with anyone involved in the finances for a program and they reviewed the expenses and provided proof for them. He had never seen that in any other ministry he had been involved in. He also said if they don't spend all the money designated for a particular project, they return the funds.

Money has never been a central focus in my life or ministry. My parents taught me how to handle money though. A friend once said to me, "When there is a problem and money is a solution and you have that

76

money, if you can resolve the problem, you don't even think, you do it." While I am sure I could critique him on that phrase, he showed wisdom. Money is a tool, but it is also a marker of the heart. Paul expressed the heart of the ministry. Money was not their treasure.

One of the challenges for MAST was that it needed to overcome the differences in how Bible translation projects were owned by the church. Communities knew of other translation models and most often, Bible translators were paid by a Western organization. We do not do that because we have a different model. When a Bible translation takes a lifetime to complete, that asks a translator for something different than asking them to be involved for a few days or weeks at a time. Through the change, we had many conversations about money. Some conversations were good and others were explanatory. Some conversation even showed negative motivation. What I heard from Paul was not only good, it was also needed in order to do what I hoped—to find a way to multiply our efforts and strategize how to engage church networks in a different way so we could do more. Paul expressed enough to show me the partners' hearts who served in excellence. Nothing more was needed. I wanted to work with them because they were good and godly men doing all they could to serve the Kingdom of God.

We tried MAST, shared what we did, and learned from one another. I listened to the ministries the group of leaders with humble facilities engaged in. It was dozens of church plants, hundreds of people being discipled and a radio ministry among other things. The group envisioned building a training facility for low-income people to participate in discipleship similar to those of seminaries without tuition costs. Throughout the week, we spoke about how to engage MAST in a new way—one that trained leaders who could go into communities and teach people. We also spoke about engaging the deaf community and someday reaching out to neighboring countries, and perhaps exploring ministries like radio.

By the last morning, several things happened. First, we had a meeting about finance of our time together because I provided the funds for our travel in and out of the country, as well as the entire duration of our stay. Leaders gave me a folder with a spreadsheet, the receipts, and returned cash, exactly as they had described their process. Second, they drafted survey questions for six languages in areas they planned to visit in upcoming months. The questions were meant to ask leaders in those communities if they needed a Bible translated in their language. The questions looked as good as I saw in organized Bible translation efforts. Third, they committed to start those languages and asked if we could help them with transportation into the villages.

That became one of a few locations that sparked a changing model of existence. That became an exploration of multipliers and a strategy of giving away everything we had. Imagine a partner who could learn what we do, engage the communities they know best, and do it for hundreds of dollars instead of thousands. What could that do for Bible translation?

Since that time, RCC church has continued to work and send pastors to neighboring villages, but now they have also extended into neighboring countries. In Bible translation efforts, here are a few things we have done together:

- They initiated six languages for Bible translation, and some are nearing completion of the New Testaments at the time of this writing.
- They developed a team of more than thirty leaders to travel with Robert to the Democratic Republic of Congo and they held the largest translation event we know of in history. They even initiated ten New Testaments and they completed the drafting at various stages within two weeks.
- They partnered with us to create a new program to teach MAST over the radio and have found and initiated four more languages in Uganda.
- They are teaching us the potential of television and how we might reach more of the region in that way.
- They have initiated a sign language Bible translation that is progressing quickly and it may be the fastest one on record for a completing a New Testament.
- They engaged in our SUN program (explained in later chapters) and Uganda is the first nation to implement the program and have it spread around the entire country.

What can humility, obedience, sacrifice, faith, and vision do? It can multiply. I cannot write this chapter without writing about Pastor Elisha. He is a man of faith behind all the effort and while I know he would be very happy to read this chapter without his name mentioned, he was the one behind every step. He attended the celebration of the five hundredth anniversary of the Ninety-Five Thesis. Pastor Elisha heard about Bible translation then. He signed up to learn more information. Out of about forty people I contacted, he was the only one who responded back. Having no time and no knowledge of who I was or how any of this might work, Pastor Elisha stepped out in faith knowing God needed it done. Pastor Elisha continues to do that today, and you can see it in what has transpired in a short amount time. Pastor Elisha is key to this region in all of the bullet points above and continues to find more ways to push ministry as far as God will allow him.

BEYOND MAST

As much as we have seen MAST impact individuals, churches, communities, and Bible translation, no one sits around Wycliffe Associates basking in the joy of the amazing amount of work God has given to us. So far, we have seen more than 1,800 languages engage in MAST, as well as hundreds of churches worldwide, and dozens of Bible translation organizations. We have also reached dozens of deaf people groups and seen some amazing firsts in Bible translation. The prevailing attitude, however, is that we hope to do more. Of course, doing more starts with a provision from God, but by faith, we believe we are called to do more.

Through several meetings—formal and informal—Wycliffe Associates' leadership began to look at the size of the task ahead. The vision is to see a Bible in every language by 2025. It has pushed us beyond our own limits, so we've asked, "What else can we do and how can we prepare for this?" The concept of growth started to emerge along with the word "multiplier." We analyzed the numbers of need with the numbers of growth necessary and realized that in order to see Vision 2025 accomplished on our terms, we needed more. A multiplication of effort was needed. A multiplication of partners. A multiplication of ownership. A multiplication of programs. From that understanding, came a restructuring in our organization. Strategic Programs became a department and was tasked with creating multiplication programs. Here are some of those programs:

Translation Education for National Training (TENT)-- A "train-the-trainers" concept through a three-day planned curriculum to teach leaders how to train others in accelerated, church-owned, Bible translation methodology.

STRIKE — A program designed to integrate into the existence of seminaries by providing short seminar trainings to full curriculum and degree programs.

Great Commission Bible Translation Network (GCBTN) — Through short conference events, gathering a network of leaders within a region who are interested in learning about Bible translation and initiating work through their influence and networks.

Radio — A program designed through curriculum-based instruction that is broadcast over radio, through YouTube channels, and on podcasts to introduce individuals, and churches, to Bible translation. Radio also has broadcasts that support ongoing work in Bible translation that links to a variety of other multiplier programs, such as TENT, and heavier facilitated programs like MAST.

Ongoing National Education (ONE) — A program designed through curriculum-based instruction to foster individual and small group facilitation from a gateway language facilitator into minority translation efforts, continuing to support the translator in their work. This program is a process multiplier to encourage continued work after a variety of events, such as MAST, Radio, and TENT initiation.

Checking Help Encouraging Completions (CHEC)—A program designed to revive stalled, abandoned, or failed projects in various Bible translation models by engaging the language groups where they are in current methodology and transitioning them toward church-owned, accelerated methodology. This program directly focuses on the completion of New Testaments and initiates Old Testament translations to produce full Bible translations.

Zonal Impact Program (ZIP)—A multiplier program designed to limit Wycliffe Associates involvement, aside from training and formation of activity through vision-casting, from the beginning. The creation of a "zone" starts with finding a local church partner who wants to influence dozens, up to hundreds, of languages in a region. The goal is to offer up methodology, but to then move them toward a visionary-based model that assists them in initiating translation in their own context through their own independence.

COMMON CHARACTERISTICS AND MEASURES

- All multipliers impact by increasing partnerships, methods and/or completions of Scripture.
- Partnership multipliers have common characteristics that include gathering visionary leaders

with influence and initiating direct starts of Scripture.

- Process and methods multiplier programs decrease costs while increasing ownership, which expresses stronger discipleship.
- Completion multiplier programs transition prior mentorship toward church-owned Bible translation methodologies for increased opportunity for church decision-making that revives and/or accelerates completions.
- All multipliers provide relationships that foster ownership, while maintaining fellowship so we are networked and providing outcome data in all directions.

BIBLICAL FOUNDATION

Acts 2 states, "They devoted themselves to the apostles' teaching and to fellowship, to the breaking of bread and to prayer. Everyone was filled with awe at the many wonders and signs performed by the apostles. All the believers were together and had everything in common. They sold property and possessions to give to anyone who had need. Every day they continued to meet together in the temple courts. They broke bread in their homes and ate together with glad and sincere hearts, praising God and enjoying the favor of all the people. And the Lord added to their number daily those who were being saved."

Characteristics

- Fellowship

- Everything in common
- They sold property and possessions to give to anyone who had a need
- Continued to meet together
- Favor of all the people
- Added to their number daily

REFLECTIVE QUESTIONS

- Fellowship—who has God put us in relationship with?
- Everything in common—who has a shared burden?
- They sold property and possessions to give to anyone who had need—who has ownership burden, including finances?
- Continued to meet together—who coordinates with us strategically in detail?
- Favor of all the people—who can go beyond our fellowship?
- Added to their number daily—who can add to the numbers?

SUMMARY STATEMENT

A multiplier should be a fellowship of people who have a common desire to translate God's Word, who are willing to contribute, and who coordinate and expand their fellowship to include others in rapid growth.

ANALYSIS OF KEY WORDS

The most interesting part of this word comparison is that the word didn't exist in the dictionary at that time. In further research, this word first appeared in English around the early 1800s but was primarily used for military functioning. It's hard to imagine how one of today's common words was not in use. One could ask, "What role does strategy have in mission's work today? The answer is the formation of use — battle. We are in a battle and we should not forget that we are waging war against Scripture poverty.

A LOOK AT KEY(ED) WORDS

From: Elisha Kakwere
Sent: Thursday, November 30, 2017 9:10 AM
To: Dan Kramer
Subject: Re: Introduction to Wycliffe associates

Hello Dan, greetings to you in Jesus name.

I was so happy to receive this email after I attended the Wittenberg Congress in Berlin 2017, which was a huge blessing to me.

We are also believing God to attend the Synergize 2018 in Orlando FL. Just waiting for our invitations for me and my other pastor.

Concerning opportunity to help reach the unreached with a mission to plant churches and help them to access a Scripture in their language, our ministry is seriously praying for that.

We are involved in planting churches in villages and town here in Central and East Africa. The work has just started but we are already having 34 churches.

Next year we are targeting 10 churches planted.

Our vision now is to establish a regional Bible training center, focused on missions and church planting. This will help us plant more intentional, healthy churches in the region. This is where we need much of your partnership support.

Secondly, we also have a plan to translate a Bible commentary and a study Bible in a local language. This is because we have here about 2 languages which use one Bible since they can heal and read. But they cannot refer anywhere. This commentary and study Bible will be helping 2 major tribes in Uganda called Banyankore / Bakiga.

Please, am very much interested in further conversation about that. Thanks a lot.

Elisha Kakwerere
Senior Pastor
Rukungiri community church
Amaziba ministries.

Response from Dan:

Dear Elisha,

Thank you so much for your response and for the details about you and your mission—amazing and wonderful! Let me suggest two things to offer to you and then some more details to what I think may coordinate mutually between us.

1. If you are coming to Orlando in late January and you can make even a few hours of time to visit Wycliffe Associates, I would love the opportunity to meet with you. The time of this conference is one of our busiest with our planning meetings, but we would make something work if that were possible.

2. I have a planned trip to Nigeria in late Febru-

ary. If I could plan a time to visit you (assuming you are located in Uganda) to see the ministry and collaborate or even set something up in a project form, I would like to offer a time of March 5-9.

Here are some thoughts on how I think we might mutually help one another in our common mission:

- If you are developing a training center, I would love to offer the ability to first teach training courses on our methodologies and tools for Bible translation and then allow them to be under your established leaders for taking over the teaching of those tools for the future.

- If you are already translating materials, we would love to partner in teaching you the methodology (with the leaders of your choice) that we have seen has greatly accelerated translation techniques that save both time and money.

- I would also like to discuss the opportunity for the use of common resources (our notes and your notes) being openly shared for all on whatever mutual resources (websites) we have for distribution, whether these are oral, written or sign language communities that they need to go to.

- I would be very interested in taking the above points into all the languages that you encounter and engaging the church (even as it grows) in how to own the Bible translation process.

If it is better to arrange a skype meeting to discuss these things but am both excited and intrigued by what God may be able to do through partnership.

Blessings,
Dan Kramer

CHAPTER NINE

It's About Time

"Time is an illusion."
— **Albert Einstein**

Key Word: Time

Webster 1828: A particular portion or part of duration, whether past, present or future

Google 2020: the indefinite continued progress of existence and events in the past, present, and future regarded as a whole

Noted Differences:
- Portion versus indefinite continued
- "regarded as a whole"

Location: Delta Airlines

It is one thing to hear the words "Thank you for your status," from an airline steward when checking in for a flight, it is another to hear someone say, "Thank you for living on our planes." I have often heard from those who travel that they would like two inventions to be made—a transporter and a time machine. In a sense, that has already happened with air travel provided in our generation. I recall landing in Los Angeles and the captain saying it was eleven in the morning. I know how time zones work, but I was still stunned. I thought, "I left Sidney, Australia at eleven this morning." As much as we can mathematically calculate what is going on, it really is amazing to be able to travel across time zones.

Time has always been precious to me, so it became one of the foundations of MAST methodology. We wanted to accelerate getting Scripture to others.

I was a runner and runners care about time. I was also a teacher and teachers are sensitive to time, well beyond the thought of summer vacations. "How long is my time for instruction?" is a common thought in a teacher's mind. What are the curriculum goals over the duration of weeks that I want to see achieved in students? What is the ratio of growth over time that these students have been influenced? There are countless measurements for time. I also come from a time-obsessed culture. "Time is money" is a common phrase. Any westerner can count the number of clocks in multiple rooms in their home and find more than one device to tell time. Our obsession has affected our subconscious and we can see it in our habits. We change lanes at stop lights based on which car to get behind to save time. When we do look at a clock, we often glance at our phones to verify it is correct. We are obsessed, but beyond the obsession, does time matter?

One hundred and fifty thousand people die every day. Of that number, it is estimated that somewhere between fifteen to thirty percent of them are Christians, but that depends on if you choose to separate evangelical faiths. It is also estimated that up to fifteen percent of the world's population has no access to Scripture in their language. Does time matter to them?

MAST was designed to save time. It was also designed to have a true measurement of completion. One of the first critical comments regarding MAST was, "Because it is so fast, can it be good quality?" While I understood the question and valued the conversation, the measurement was immediately based on unfair acceptance of assumption. Good translation takes a long time. That was a leap in assumption that up until a certain day had not been proven true at all. In fact, in the larger scope of Bible translation, the work of those pushing change showed otherwise, and their timelines could be easily constructed. The exploration of time-lines is not intended to be a debate between methods or skepticism, it is intended to pause and reflect on our attitudes about time.

When we don't understand something, we tend to believe it will take a long time to get to the conclusion. Think about what you choose not to do because it will take time. One example is not reading instruction man-uals, no matter how easy they are to read. Our time-ob-sessed culture has put general assumptions into what time is, what time can control, and what time mandates of us. That is a problem. We think we own time. We think we control it. We think we can make assumptions about it and determine what will and will not take time. Is that not the same thing evolution tried to pursue in falsely educating society? We refuse what is evidenced through Scripture and what God shows us in the quali-ties of what is around us (Rom. 1:20) and then say "it's complex" offering a solution of time to explain it away. The work of God demands that the time in the work also belongs to God.

MAST Methodology

Time in MAST has two primary functions—controlled and contained. The controlled timing is in the first four steps of drafting. In brain theory, when we want to use short term memory and long term attachment, we need to tap into both. To do so, we have to acknowledge the brain's efficiency. Brains consume a lot of information on conscious and subconscious levels. Some of that is never seen, such as regulated breathing, background noise, surrounding visual elements, colors, lighting, etc. At the same time, our brains consume information that is both new and/or old. In doing an activity, such as translation, it is ideal to quickly move information through short term memory. If information is not moved fast enough, the brain, in its efficiency, will start to discard information so it can continue to consume the next conscious thought while still performing subconscious duties. That means, you have five to seven minutes to consume new information and about ten minutes to do something with it. This is why MAST drafting steps are fast. This is also why MAST drafting steps are time-controlled and give us a measurement for time. It is also why blind drafting works; the brain still holds the information at the time for capturing naturalness in language.

The second half of MAST is checking. In this phase, we get as much time as we need with no sense of push at all. We have captured language in such a way in drafting, and because the language is alive and fresh in the brain, it is easy to begin the checking process. That is where the phrase "good translation takes time" doesn't fit with brain theory. When a method claims that good practice includes setting aside a piece of translation for a long period of time before bringing it back to the table for some form of checking, the method dismisses functional realities of time. There is no way to say that work that sat for a long time before any form of checking was a good process. Reviving prior work to reflect on and improve is not impossible; however, it takes a revisit to what was happening in the brain at the time of the work which requires more time. The phrase "good translation takes time" becomes a self-fulfilling prophecy.

A key sentence to review is: The work of God demands that the time in the work also belongs to God. If we don't believe that, we are fooling ourselves. In the chapter on faith, I referred to the gap. Time is one of those things underlying God's ownership that we do not acknowledge. We acknowledge time when we pray for a loved one who is ill. We acknowledge time when we pray for things in duration, like pregnancy or time to heal. Yet, we rarely pray for elements of time in the day to day management of a task. We rarely pray for time that sounds like, "Lord, give me more time today to do what I need to do." Imagine if we prayed for our time in Bible translation. That is the attitude that MAST desires to have in relation to time. Translation is not a recipe or a mathematical calculation, it's a God-honoring task that reaches people who matter and are dying every day.

BIBLICAL FOUNDATION JOSHUA 10
THE DAY TIME STOOD STILL

In the middle of a battle, imagine the prayer to ask for more time. It's not only the sense of request that is amazing, it's the sense of getting the job done. There are elements in this that every Christian needs to comprehend, revive, and use:

- A sense of urgency
- A sense of completion
- A sense of request (we serve a big God)
- An amazing result
- God controls time

Imagine if these five principles were applied to any mission. How much more effective would a mission be? Would we be?

ANALYSIS OF KEY WORD

The words between these two definitions show a fascinating contrast. One segments time into portions, and the other eludes to time as indefinite. This reminds me of Einstein's quote: "Time is an illusion." To our God, existing outside of time and creating it for our human existence; I have to agree.

A LOOK AT KEY(ED) WORDS

We don't have time for that right now.

CHAPTER TEN
All Means All

> "When you don't know to raise love to everyone, you fall in love with one—yourself."
> — **P.S. Jagadeesh Kumar**

Key Word: All

Webster 1828: 1. Everyone, or the whole number of particulars. 2. The whole quantity, extent, duration, amount, quality, or degree.

Google 2020: used to refer to the whole quantity or extent of a particular group or thing

Noted Change:
- Absence of duration, amount, quality, degree

Location: Southeast Asia, November 2014, Orlando, Florida, 2016, and Asuncion, Paraguay, January 2017

W ithin a few minutes of my arrival I met another Wycliffe Associates staff member and an urgent plea, "We have to pray!"

Jet-lagged, as usual, I chuckled then responded, "Of course, we can pray."

I was redirected to the event coming the next day. "You don't understand, the two language groups gathered are illiterate." The groups didn't read or write in the source language. That certainly changed things. I thought about how to adjust, but was interrupted with more information. "It's worse than that. The languages we are translating to have never been written before."

The next morning, while continuing to pray without ceasing, I approached the groups for some introductory statements. I did the best I could to stall for more time so I could think. I asked everyone to introduce themselves. Naively, thinking this was helpful, I heard testimonies that only increased the urgency of the situation.

"My name is Dorcas and I am a pastor in my village. There are no male Christians. In my community, I encounter many females. In my culture, as a minority, you are allowed to have two children. The first can be a boy or a girl. The second, if you haven't had a boy, is left to starve if it is a girl," she paused. "My country allows this. The culture allows this. Everything tells these women it is okay. They only speak their minority language. I need Scripture in this language."

If I had any thoughts of trying to explain that MAST had never done oral language translation and easing out of the room with apologies for misunderstanding their needs, that was no longer possible. I found myself in front of the room, whispering to God, "What do I do?" On cue, I was reminded that language is a path of skills—listening, speaking, writing, and reading. They didn't have writing and reading. They had speaking and listening, but it was at different levels of bilingualism. I remembered a fifth language skill. At every stage of growth, thinking skill is a base for language and we can use thought fragments in the brain to get it done. I put my hand in my pocket, which grazed my cell phone. "We can capture it on a cell phone recorder," I thought.

On that day, in fragmented form, we began oral language translation. Not because we knew what to do or because we were so well-experienced in MAST, but because we responded to an urgent need in faith. I prayed that day. I thanked God for the progress of anything positive that happened in the room. I also joked with God and asked Him not to do that to me again. He did anyway. I sincerely asked God to, "Give me the eyes of preparation for whom I will encounter in the future." Coming out of that prayer, I knew we would translate for the deaf.

Two years later, Ashley, a daughter of my key staff member for supporting all our leaders, visited me in my office. More importantly though, Ashley was a former Sunday School student from my home church in Michigan. Ashley very boldly said, "We need to do something for deaf people." I looked back at her with a smirk. "Did a nineteen-year-old just come in here telling me what my job was?" I thought to myself. She did though. I challenged her right back and asked her to help me assemble the first experiment for using MAST Bible translation for the deaf. She accepted the task and weeks later we had four individuals, who were deaf, from the United States to try methodology we named Deaf Owned Translation (DOT).

A person who was trained in traditional Bible translation methodology for the deaf was in the experiment room. Mirta, a leader in Paraguay, came to watch. I was terrified because it was our first experiment and she had decades of experience. Mirta sat quietly at the corner of the table the entire week. For the first couple days, I didn't know if she loved what we were doing or hated it. From my view, after only a few hours, I could see we had the same potential to reach people who were deaf for Bible translation as the oral language groups. Mid-week, Mirta asked me to talk to her. She had some notes written on small pieces of paper and napkins. She asked, "Do you think we could gather groups from each of these countries and bring them to Paraguay to try this?" She had seven countries listed. All I could say was, "I think you are more crazy than me! Yes, let's do it!"

In January 2017, we hosted, to my knowledge, what was the largest deaf translation event in history. We gathered teams from seven nations and I found myself in the front of a room speaking English, which was translated into Spanish and Portuguese, then further translated into seven sign languages throughout the room. It was one of the most amazing teaching moments of my entire life. The story didn't end there—it began there. It wasn't just the start for DOT, it started another program called Symbolic Universal Notation (SUN).

Out of the many participants in our DOT event, there was one woman who could not translate. I got to spend a few minutes with her and discovered it was due to her lack of education in her sign language. I tried to teach her for a little while, but it became embarrassing for her to be pulled from the group, so I stopped. That experience forced me to ask the question, "How many deaf people in the world do not know sign language?" The answer, I discovered, was a majority of them. Of the nearly seventy-million people who are deaf in the world, fifty-six million never learn a sign language. We had a responsibility for that population.

If Scripture is for everyone, how could we give them access to God's Word?

The path of this story could easily create multiple chapters and another book. The SUN program was designed to teach the deaf without sign language acquisition and the deaf-blind how to access God's Word. In short, SUN is a language created for a literacy program that transcends timelines of any literacy program in existence. At the time of writing this book, we have seen the language used to create transformation in eight countries. We have seen the language be used to create worship music in Burkina Faso to include people who are deaf into a wider church worship. We have seen the language used to bring salvation decisions to a deaf and blind man who was raised by his Muslim family. Only God could create a situation where a deaf and blind son could be the light of truth in a Muslim home.

Today, SUN is a program that expresses that Wycliffe Associates believes all means all. In other words, when we talk about a Bible in every language, we consider audience and that includes those who write and read Scripture, those who speak and listen to Scripture, those who are deaf and watch Scripture, and those whose language is only in their own minds.

BIBLICAL FOUNDATION MARK 7 AND JOHN 9

Imagine a deaf person you knew told the story of Mark 7. They told you that a man took a deaf person aside and he put his fingers in his ears, spit, and touched the deaf person's tongue and then looked up and commanded, "Be opened!" Then the deaf man could hear. How could we comprehend that? How do we begin to feel the emotion of that joy? Or should we, instead, be like those who are in disbelief, such as the skeptics in John 9 when Jesus healed a blind man?

I have heard people describe our programs as miraculous. I have heard this about our English programs, about MAST, DOT, and SUN as well. I actually do not know how to receive and process it. To believe that I am somewhere in the middle of so many miraculous moments is humbling to levels of frightening. Yet, when we see people who are deaf receive Scripture, we can understand the phrase, "be opened!" Just as the life of that person in Mark 7 was changed from completely unexpected events, so are the people being touched by SUN.

ANALYSIS OF KEY WORDS

The absence of some of the words in the modern definition is a little surprising considering that we are such a measured and evaluative society. The absence of duration, amount, quality, and degree are measurements that seem to take the word "all" to a higher level of inclusion. Today, when we pretend to be more enlightened in our inclusivity, I find it fascinating that we see important terms like "all" become less measured. Instead we define "all" as a particular rather than a whole of all the particulars. That is a dramatic and distinctive difference. It's equivalent to saying, "all in a group" versus "all the groups." In our society's push for "all," are we really considering all or are we segmenting and dividing? If we are dividing, we have to ask ourselves why.

A LOOK AT KEY(ED) WORDS

Mark Chapter 1 in SUN:

CHAPTER ELEVEN

I Didn't Do it

"I had a dream about you. We were actors in a horror movie and I was hunting you down with a knife. When I finally cornered you, the director yelled "Cut"... What? I can't be blamed for following instructions."

— **Georgia Saratsioti**, *Dreaming is for lovers*

Key Word: Blameless

Webster 1828: Without fault; innocent; guiltless; not meriting censure

Google 2020: Innocent of wrongdoing

Note Change:
- Absence of fault, guilt, censure
- Innocent broadly versus specific

Location: Earth 2014-2020 or Since Eden

It is amazing to live in a time where innovation in Bible translation has been met with such favor, acceptance, and freedom from political strife. Wait! That didn't happen!

It would be nice to believe that ministry is full of Christians who harmoniously work together in utopia. If that were true, we could look at the names of churches each week and note the absence of a denominational marker in many of them. The human experience within a spiritual endeavor is challenging. Mistakes are made. Feelings are hurt. Arguments happen. Disagreements occur. That is as old as establishing the church in the New Testament. We can see them as negative situations, but we can also see them as opportunities. Opportunities to express the fruits of the Spirit in our work. Opportunities to do our best at being blameless.

MAST was primarily met with two types of people—one was skeptical and the other was curious. Both types of people can be good. Beyond those, other opinions and agendas have transpired, but I can't answer those. I cannot respond to accusations, false evaluations, and judgments intended to discourage, steal resources, or completely end MAST. As far as quotes like "MAST Bibles will send people to hell," I can only testify to that falsehood based on the hundreds of testimonies of transformed lives around the world.

MAST is not removed from politics, division, or human sinfulness. Our job—my personal job—is to evaluate that in myself and encourage staff members, translators, and partners to do the same. We do it by openly using the term "blameless" and evaluating one another with the question: "Are we blameless in this decision or situation?" Of course, there are times we are not blameless, but we also find times to evaluate ourselves before we get to that point. As you might imagine, we can find times for reflection and growth. It is an effort we must continue to make. We must continue to explore and dwell on in our prayer, meditation, and work.

MAST is constantly met with skeptical and curious audiences at events and within communities and churches, as well as organizations we cross paths with. We understand that MAST is an interruptive process to what has been done in past methodologies and it will create change. As the program grows, the intensity of harsh responses can increase versus decrease. One of the ways we have learned to handle harsh responses is through open-handed Biblical treatment.

BIBLICAL FOUNDATION

One of the best ways to understand Jesus is by reading His words. Precise, cutting, and direct are some traits we might associate with His speech. Mentoring, wise, and loving are other words to associate with Him. Think about Jesus' ministry once it became known in society. He faced challenging situations. Some of the people deemed "religious" confronted Jesus several times and tried to trick, trap, and thwart Him. Taking His responses to each of those situations and lining them up one after another is a great study. You will see that Jesus either didn't respond or he replied with a question.

Other people approached Jesus and did not believe or understand; they were wanters and doubters. Some wanted to understand, so they asked Jesus, "How can

I be born a second time?" Other people doubted Jesus could do what He said He could do.

Thomas was one of those doubters. In situations of want and doubt, Jesus showed people. For Thomas, he made it more than visual. Thomas touched reality. That is our answer to the skeptics and doubters of MAST. We say, "Come and see. See all you want. Critique all you want. Evaluate the program. Give us feedback. We will do our best to listen because your heart seeks what is needed.

In MAST, DOT, SUN, and Other Programs

If you are a doubter and a wanter, with a truly interested heart, come and see. Likewise, we are all responsible to do the same. None of the programs created for Bible translation were done without going to see. None of the programs created for Bible translation were done in isolation or ignored past histories of translation. None of the programs created for Bible translation were created without the highest level of expertise from other methodologies involved.

Analysis of Key Word

Ungodly culture will always move away from self-reflection that measures us to a godly standard. That provides our comfort and control over having to admit to our sin. If you compare these definitions, the modern one is a term that sounds more like a court decision than self-reflection.

A Look at Key(ed) Words

For the sake of nondiscouragement, I chose not to include emails that demonstrate behaviors expressed above. However, there are many.

CHAPTER TWELVE
Who Cares More?

"I'd rather make a show 100 people need
to see, than a show that 1000 people
want to see."

— **Joss Whedon**

Key Word: Quality

Webster 1828: Property; that which belongs to a body
or substance, or can be predicated of it

Google 2002: the standard of something as measured
against other things of a similar kind; the degree of
excellence of something.

Noted Change: What do you see?

Location: Undisclosed

I interviewed Jessica [name changed for safety], about
the transformation that took place since the beginning of translation efforts. What I heard amazed me.

Chapter ten talked about some of the challenges in
relationship to people who are skeptics to MAST and

those who were curious to see more. The amount of people who wanted to see the process for themselves did not stop the debate or fear for quality. Nor did I ever want it to. Unfortunately, open hands with open invitations don't always lead to a resolution. That's okay too, and my ideal desire is to keep learning from one another without distraction. One of those areas of discussion is and should always be quality.

One of the primary differences in MAST methodology is ownership. Going back to the original conversation that ignited all of this, Jeewan asked for something that could empower nationals in their ownership. MAST provides this through the translation process, but it also allows quality to be part of the process for the local church because it's not under the control of a western organization. I have engaged in hundreds of conversations with donors, translators, Bible translation leaders, radio interview hosts, and seminary instructors, and a common question always emerges. "Can the church in the village really determine the quality of Scripture?"

I am going to take this question out of context for a moment and put it into another one that plays off my Detroit heritage. "Can the Japanese really take the idea of car production and produce a car of quality?" The context of the question is ridiculous. The context of the question in the 1950s had to be asked, joked about, and dismissed. If you can understand the complexity of putting together a car from scratch, please ask yourself, "What is it humans cannot learn to do?"

MAST was born out of an education process not a linguistic analysis process, so you can understand the layers of quality. First, quality begins from within. Even in drafting, we have some steps in the process that demand discipline and lay a foundation for good practice. The consume step builds context. Then the verbalize step activates the brain. The step of chunking follows brain process to make the task right-sized while holding contextual understanding. The step of blind drafting forces naturalness. Without these items in drafting, quality is immediately diminished.

After that foundation for drafting, MAST has four layers of quality that immediately follow drafting. Self-checking uses a comparable analysis of a trusted source text next to new text. Peer checking multiplies the amount of eyes on the draft, which is just like trading your paper in a classroom. As a teacher—MAST facilitation lead—we can put a higher functioning peer with a lower function worker at any given point. Some individuals are stronger in language skill while others are stronger in theology. Coupling two individuals into a team not only improves translation, but it also improves the two individuals. Keyword checking is the hold on scriptural integrity by word-based meaning and it is met with contextual wrapping. In combination, these two steps solidify the language, so there is only a small chance of error. When these steps are owned by the church and followed with an obedience to the task, we see excellent translation happen fast.

Beyond MAST's checking steps, there is also audience exposure. People who are concerned about the quality ask: "Who is trained in the room?" They want to know who is trained in theology, trained in languages like Greek and Hebrew, and trained in the native language.

We approach this question and ask a different question for every evaluation. We ask, "What can you do?" In other words, we look for who is in the room, what their skill set is, and how that skill can best contribute to the task. This simple flip allows us to then ask, "Where do we have strengths and weaknesses in the translation process?" Often, we can group people who have strong backgrounds in theology with those who have a weaker background in it. If we cannot do this, we increase the team's resources. The process for a translation event begins with student assessments, which are conducted on the first day of every workshop.

On day two of every MAST workshop, we initiate an authentic assessment rubric development. It is a detailed list of what it takes for Scripture to be high quality. We have collected hundreds of the rubrics and we could absolutely make a list of qualities for evaluation, but we teach ownership with MAST and ask the church to develop a process. We compare that process to what we know should be present in translation, too. That way we can express quality measures in our own terms. These rubrics then become lists every translator can use as a reference guide to check each verse. The qualities within the rubrics are well above and beyond any organizational standard of checking.

Wycliffe Associates aspires to provide and invest in a set of material that is copyright free and available for use in thirty-eight major languages. The set of material includes Scripture source text that is free for use under a share-alike copyright, along with translation notes, keyword resources, and higher level thinking questions for comprehension. In time, the content will also include pictures for key words that are often outside of cultural context, maps, and resources for biblical languages. The material contribute to quality translation because they provide insight to those who may not be theologically trained.

We strive to evaluate our partnerships, as well as ourselves, when it comes to our Bible translation efforts. From experienced Bible translation partners, we have collected testimonies about MAST in various forms. We have completed a variety of our own internal studies, which have included well over a dozen Bible translation consultants (early on as we were developing MAST), comparable testing to other methodologies (including the use of machine-driven translation), tweaks in our own methodology, and blind studies where we had people compare source texts that were deemed high quality to MAST translated materials.

During my conversation with Jessica, I asked her something more than correctness and quality in Scripture. I asked her to move away from the human endeavor of exploring quality and talk to me about transformation. Scripture shows us what the impact should be—transformation. Jessica told me stories about four different language groups we both knew. I saw amazing transformation results, as evidenced in one of the response forms below. Above all measurements of quality, this is the outcome we should seek.

A LOOK AT KEY(ED) WORDS

One of the Four Languages Shared from Jessica

Biblical Outcomes Rubric for Measuring Impact in Scripture Translation

Language: Undisclosed for safety

Location: Undisclosed

Type of translation: Oral

Current Scope of Work: Partial completion of New Testament

Outcome: The Bible is profitable for teaching (2 Timothy 3:16)

Measure(s): Has the church used translated Scripture for teaching? YES

How is the church using what was translated for teaching?

What was the result of that teaching?

There has been witnessed use of Scripture teaching in the fellowship and in small group teaching, resulting in new believers. The testimony given by the national program manager is "this is the most active group in teaching before a finished new testament".

Outcome: The Bible is instruction to give hope (Romans 15:4, Psalms 119:9)

Measure: Have you seen the people receiving Scripture increase in hope? YES

How has this translated Scripture inspired hope in people or the wider community?

The "Ghost Doctor" (medicine man) heard that Jesus can heal, so they came to hear about Jesus. As they did, they understood that Jesus gives hope and new life meaning and they became Christian with many others.

Outcome: The Bible accomplishes God's Purpose (Isaiah 55:11, Joshua 1:8)

Measures: Since obtaining Scripture, have you seen the church grow in accomplishing God's purpose? YES

How would the church define God's purpose?

How has the church seen God's purpose impacted by the newly translated Scripture?

They have developed new group leaders and teachers and have an expanding church.

Outcome: The Bible increases faith (Romans 10:17)

Measure: Have you seen an increase of faith in the church since planting Scripture? YES

How has faith increased from Scripture in your church/community?

They have decided to expand the church by growth and developing more independent self-supported fellowships—by faith.

Outcome: The Bible discerns the heart (Hebrews 4:12-14)

112

Measure: Have you seen increased discernment in the people who have obtained Scripture? YES

From a number of individuals, how has discernment been influenced by Scripture?

In the sense of cultural impact, they have changed some views on treatment of females and including them and eliminating negative responses that are not godly.

Outcome: The Bible provides healing (Proverbs 4:20-23)

Measure: Have you seen an increase in healing (emotionally, spiritually, health issues) since Scripture has been translated? YES

What are some examples of healing people have had from the translated Scripture?

Most strongly expressed in the sense of emotional healing, breaking boundaries of fear.

Outcome: The Bible revives the soul (Psalms 19:7-11)

Measure: Have you seen any sense of revival in the community or individuals from Scripture translation? YES

What are some examples of people having had their soul revived from the translated Scripture?

Increased comprehension gives respect and leads towards a desire of wanting to serve.

Outcome: The Bible distinguishes good from evil (Hebrews 5:14)

Measure: Have you seen an increase of understanding from good vs evil since Scripture has been translated? YES

What are some changes in activity that you have noticed from Biblical influence?

Reduction of gambling.

Outcome: The Bible gives testimony to truth (John 17:17)

Measure: Has there been an increased witness of Jesus since Scripture? YES

In the form of church growth

Outcome: The Bible is a way toward understanding salvation (2 Peter 3:15-16)

Measure: Have you seen salvation decisions as a result from Scripture translation? YES

114

How many salvation decisions have happened from Scripture influence?

Over 20, probably close to 30.

Outcome: The Bible provides spiritual growth (2 Timothy 4:1-7)

Measure: Have you seen spiritual growth in individuals, churches or communities since the Scripture has been brought to them? YES

What evidence have you seen of spiritual growth from translated Scripture?

Increase in worship (even openly) and an increase in direct Bible study

CHAPTER THIRTEEN
The Day The Earth Shook

"Urgency and despair don't get along well."
> — **N.K. Jemisin**

"Delays and laziness are the two great gulfs in which multitudes of souls are drowned and perish."
> — **John Fox, Time and the End of Time**

"I have been impressed with the urgency of doing. Knowing is not enough; we must apply. Being willing is not enough; we must do."
> — **Leonardo da Vinci**

Key Word: Urgency

Webster 1828: Pressure; importunity; earnest solicitation; Pressure of necessity

Google 2020: importance requiring swift action. An earnest and persistent quality; insistence.

Noted Differences:

- Loss of Pressure
- Loss of Necessity
- Loss of solicitation
- Addition of Insistence
- Addition of swift action

Location: Tribuvan International Airport in Kathmandu, Nepal on April 25, 2015

I knew enough to pause and look around. I crouched down on one knee and took pictures of the people scattering across the runway in random directions. I asked God, "Why did you want me here at this moment?" I was on one of the few airplanes allowed to take off the day an 8.1 magnitude earthquake hit Nepal. Looking back, it was a rare moment in time of tragedy and isolation that really didn't make sense because most flights didn't leave. I was given just enough time to feel the situation by God allowing me to be at my airport boarding door (about to line up) and then being allowed to take off about six hours later. In those first minutes on the runway, and the few hours that passed, I couldn't help but think about the reality of the situation. I didn't know who was alive, dead, bruised, or buried. I did know that whatever work we started was more urgent than I imagined. The fragility of life struck me, not for myself, but for the many tribes and nations.

Arriving in Dubai my phone quickly connected to the internet again. Text messages and emails poured in upon internet connection and my eyes welled with tears because of people's concern for me. I stopped walking through the airport and sifted through everyone's words. I couldn't consume and still can't fully explain that moment. I slept as little as I ever had that next week. I searched through news channels to get as much detail about what continued to take place in Nepal.

My sense of urgency began that moment in the airport, but it evolved into comprehension over a few days. As the emotion of each of those moments and days converged, I found myself understanding more deeply how critical the task was. Bible translation wasn't just an urgent task to work on, it was an urgent task to complete. In other words, starting was not enough. Completion was the only thing that mattered. At the time of the earthquake, we were getting ready to bring back the people who did the first, two-week New Testament trial project. It would be their second event to strive to complete the second half of their work.

On the runway I had whispered to myself, "I am so glad the people we worked with to translate Scripture quickly already have half their New Testament." I thought about what would happen if all of those translators died. They had not died, and they further surprised everyone by gathering for a week in the days after the earthquake to complete another twenty-five percent of the New Testament translation.

There was a lot of skepticism about MAST at that time because it was very early in the endeavor and only had a few languages so far that had used the new methodology. A western mentality would call for testing. It could call for more trials. For review. For experts to weigh in on opinions. The reality is, we had a choice for MAST. We could submit it to the critics and skeptics, accept their timeline, and hold back while we waited for review, or we could approach the task with urgency. We chose the second option and there is no stronger personal story I can share that expresses my thankfulness for that.

The story continues, however, because that translation team *did* complete the New Testament and I was able to celebrate that completion high in the mountains of Nepal a few months later. To be clear, the people who read Scripture with me for Christmas in December 2014 and continued to translate through the earthquake in April 2015 celebrated in a little mountain church high in the clouds of the mountains. The roads were steep, muddy, crossed rivers, and often had no room for more than one car to pass. At some points, the non-Nepali passengers wanted to get out of the car and walk through some of the more treacherous parts of the road where we envisioned it slipping down the side of the cliff from trying to force through the mud. At other times, we were sure a wheel skipped over the edge of the road as it curved around a turn. After eighteen hours of driving the muddy road on a cliff in an imitation Jeep with failing windshield wipers, a failing horn, and a bad rear axle, I got the honor to sleep on the floor of their church and celebrate with them the next morning. During the celebration, the most defining moment for me was a little girl who couldn't walk yet. She sat on the floor in a beautiful dress. I stared at the girl thinking, "She has access Scripture for the rest of her life." The girl didn't even know about the earthquake and all the urgency a community, church and family had for her to access God's word in her native language. I'm so glad we pursued our work with urgency so that girl would grow up reading Scripture.

BIBLICAL FOUNDATION

Think of a person you know personally who has passed away. If you can recall the last conversation with that person, think about their words to you. Do you remember them? Last words are pretty impactful and are often remembered for their value of timing. In the closing chapter of Scripture we see this as well. Revelation 22 states "Behold, I am coming quickly!" Wanting to keep context to anything in Scripture that is quoted, keep in mind, this is a book of prophecy, glimpsing into the end. That timeline, whatever it is, is determined as "quick." Scripture, at several points, expressed that our days are numbered, limited, pressing, and evaluated. Imagine a parent calling a child on the phone to say, "We are coming home quickly," and then the child saying, "Oh, I thought you meant I had more time." You know how that unfolds. The tasks we are given and commanded to do are not choices of time, they are urgent demands. If we forget about the urgency, we miss the key words given to us.

ANALYSIS OF KEY WORDS

Of all the key words chosen, this is one of the more shocking ones to me. We have stolen from a larger whole for self-centered behavior. The definition removes the words "pressure," "necessity." and "solicitation." Loss of pressure demonstrates a willful neglect to surrounding. Loss of necessity demonstrates ignoring our priorities. Loss of solicitation demonstrates the admittance of needing submission. In turn, the addition of insistence replaces necessity with human pressure. The addition of swift action is good, but in the context of the modern definition, it is without humility of submission so it becomes individualized human will. It is no wonder our definition of urgency today is shrouded in selfish behaviors and decisions of personal endeavors.

A LOOK AT KEY(ED) WORDS

A letter sent to friends and family after the earthquake:

> We thank you all for your prayers! Dan is still in Nepal and was in the airport when the earthquake hit. His team is safe but need continued prayer as they work through living in the surrounding devastation and some traveling back home. I finally got word that Dan is safe this afternoon. God is so good! We continue to praise him, knowing this will bring Nepal to Christ! Dan wanted to send you all word and has emailed me an update.
>
> I LOST MY WATER BOTTLE
>
> It's so strange to think that 15 minutes ago I was drinking coffee and realizing it was time to go through security and board my plane. No rush in Kathmandu, things don't move too quickly to boarding. It was a very smooth routine through screening, and it was time to wait for the bus to come pick us up to take us to our plane.
>
> An eerie silence hushed the airport with a pause. Then a panic. The ground wasn't shaking—the whole airport was. A quick rush to the door, a few people pushed over and then masses of people spreading out over the runway with the ground still shaking. You now know what it feels like no matter how strong or weak. An earthquake real enough to shut everything down.
>
> I used to uncomfortably joke about the "earth-

quake alarms" in the places I stayed but when you look out a window and realize how bad the infrastructure is and how crowded people are within it, whatever might have been humor to ease the anxiety beneath it no longer exists.

Sitting on a bus still feeling tremors and verbal reports about fallen buildings, cracked roads, 3000 dead and it reaching to other cities in Nepal, makes it all even more real. Writing this at the airport as it's happening, what really happened I won't know but thoughts quickly go to the team I was just with from Nepal, China and Myanmar who were just trained so they could do more far reaching Bible translation programs.

In the rush to get out of the airport I lost my water bottle. Not just a water bottle but a very expensive (but often needed) UV water purifier. For a second I wanted to look for it. Yet I realized how worthless material things are. How quickly the foundations can collapse on everything a human owns.

Nepal is one big earthquake away from millions of dead. The tremors don't ease that fear of possible reality. There are 37 languages that need Gods word. How quickly do they need that to happen? As if I didn't look at what I'm doing with enough urgency, now I know how it feels.

Sincerely,

Dan Kramer

CHAPTER FOURTEEN

The Truck Driver, Rancher, and Real Estate Agent

"The mind once enlightened cannot again become dark."

— **Thomas Paine**

Key Word: Experience

Webster 1828: Trial, or a series of trials or experiments; active effort or attempt to do or to prove something, or repeated efforts. Observation of a fact or of the same facts or events happening under like circumstances

Google 2020: practical contact with and observation of facts or events. Encounter.

Noted Differences
- Absence of trial, experiment, active effort (or repeated efforts)
- Absence of attempting to prove something
- Absence of happening under like circumstances

Location: Kathmandu, Nepal in July 2009

It's nice to end where it began—Kathmandu, Nepal. While MAST began in the summer of 2014, my personal missionary journey with Wycliffe Associates begin in 2009—also in Kathmandu. I would like to end this book where I began.

I've chosen the word "experience" for this chapter because on my personal journey I was studying *Experiencing God* by Henry Blackaby when I was struggling to find what God really wanted for my life. While I believed I was doing good in my work, raising my children in a good Christian environment, and also actively serving in my church, something still felt unsettled. My sense of being right with God in terms of fully giving in to what He wanted wasn't there.

I had been going through a series of different Bible studies over a few years and purposely joined an early Saturday morning group of men who were four to six decades older than me so I could study God's Word and learn from their lives. They did not disappoint. The transparency, sharing of mistakes, devotion to prayer, and genuine calmness in their spirits of having an under-standing of God's grace and interventions in them, gave me things I still am uncovering over time. Eventually, however, *Experiencing God* was a study the entire church started. I glanced over it, but I could never fully engage for some reason. So I decided to take the book with me on my mission trip with Wycliffe Associates. Little did I know what I was getting myself into.

Of all the things you can learn from Blackaby's book, the obvious theme of "go where God is working and join Him in His work" screamed at me. "That's it! That's what's missing," I thought as I read through

125

the pages. I was living a good life and was doing good work. I just wasn't doing His work or even thinking about where He was working. Think about that for a second. Whatever we do, no matter how good the work, how often do we miss joining Him in what He is doing and where He is doing it? It shook me in the best way to realize, God determines me. I do not determine where He should meet me. It shook me in a bad way, because I read the book in Kathmandu and was rooming with a missionary who served in India.

God had placed me in a room with a man who was the same age as me, had the same number of children, and had a similar educational background. The difference was that he was a missionary working on Bible translation. God worked on me a lot and he used a book, a trip, and a roommate to further His cause.

One evening my roommate asked, "Would you like to see what I do?" He already had his laptop open and was about to show me pictures. My mind said, "Um, no thank you," because I wanted to resist what God was doing inside me. Out of politeness, however, I proceeded to look at his pictures of people he worked with, locations around India, and family celebrations. He spoke further about separated birthdays and holidays and kids in boarding schools because that was the best option available. My nervousness increased, and perhaps my naïve nature did to. I went to bed that night believing God was calling me to ministry in India. Nothing against India at all, but I was terrified! Somehow, some way, after some long prayers, I went to bed saying to God, "You are God. I am not, and I will do what you want me to do even if I don't want to do it." While I cannot give a testimony that there was relief in that prayer, I can say, it was the prayer I needed. It was the submission I had previously missed. The next morning, as I was preparing for my responsibilities, the leader of our program offered the opportunity to create the English language learning program for Wycliffe Associates.

The relevance of this story is not my sense of experience, it is experience itself that is important. The definitions provided above lay the foundation for thought in this chapter. In western culture, we use the word "experience" in terms of credentials, which often relates to resumes and job hunting. This experience has a perceived value. Perhaps that has blurred our comprehension of what experience is in God's terms. Reflect on Scripture in the sense of who was called to serve him. Reflect on experience as part of the credentials. I'm not saying experience is worthless. I'm not saying God doesn't give us experiences to develop us either. What I am saying is, God controls experience. God gives experience. God *is* experience and the closer we draw to Him, the more we experience Him.

Instead, we often create our experiences and we create our future endeavors of experience in our plans, hopes, and dreams. This is what I did. When I did that, I only had my human experiences to refer to. It created an absence of letting God lead in experiences. That created a personal void where I expressed, "There is supposed to be more in life, isn't there?" Instead of coming to terms with it, I put a perceived value on my own human experiences above God's. I distracted myself with gaining credentials and accomplishments, but I never asked God, "Is this where you want me?"

Just as society values experience for being a valuable person to draw upon, what if we were to look at experience as a thing that can only be obtained through

God? What if God was the only source of experience? How would our experiences look? Would it look like our outlines of expertise? Would it look like our resumes? Or would it look like working where He is and joining Him however, and whenever, He tells us?

BIBLICAL FOUNDATION

In 2013, I sat in Ethiopia proposing a way to learn English faster to highly educated people. While it was a serious conversation, it was not in a meeting. They asked about our credentials. I had some, but then my three other team members revealed their professional experiences. Neal was a retired truck driver. Susan was a retired real-estate agent. Lori was in her thirties and enjoyed working on a ranch. They were the English teaching team who would take on the task of teaching better and faster than they would ever imagine. The reality is, experience from prior qualifications was not needed, only experience in language. There's a difference in how we see and use the word. Experience is both historical and in the moment. God calls for us to join Him in the moment, not collect historical events. Which ones do we do?

It's not hard to comprehend the truth of this when we see who Jesus called as His disciples. It's also not hard to see the truth behind this when we think of who God called to the work of critical importance. He chose a shepherd as a king. He chose a man to build an ark when no one could conceptualize its purpose. He chose children as kings. He chose a stutterer to lead a nation and approach a king. What are the credentials of these servants? They all went where God was working, and they joined Him. They were not collecting human
128

endeavors for God to say, "Wow, you're so qualified, let me use you."

Again, I am not suggesting that education and expertise are bad things. What I am suggesting is, we often do things out of order, or in our own way, and then expect God to come into our decisions as if he is somehow responsive to us, instead of us being responsive to Him. If we were to seek what God wants in our acquisition of things, to drive that motivation for education, expertise, or anything else is simply absent of God giving it versus God directing it. If I'm critiquing anything, it is myself for having lived over a decade doing exactly that and wishing I had not. Despite that, God groomed me anyway. He knew there would come a point in time where I would experience change. I am so thankful.

My appeal to you is not about MAST—although I believe MAST is an experience where He is working. If you see it with an open heart to God, you will see His work. My appeal to you is that you experience God. It is that you have a story riddled with just that—a reflection of Him doing what He wills and you struggling to weave through it the best you can. It is my hope for myself, my children, and every Christian.

ANALYSIS OF KEY WORDS

Active effort is perhaps the largest absence between definitions. While both definitions point to facts (a good thing that I suspect will disappear over time), the sense that experience is all reflective or trends toward past tense (primarily) or a random encounter in tone should be disturbing to us. This starts to do two things. The first is that an in the moment experience is not as valuable because it was not tested over time. I find this dangerously out of line with scriptural experiences. The second is that encounter experiences sounds a bit dismissive and whimsical, which either makes them less valuable or individualized where no one can find the facts in them any longer.

A LOOK AT KEY(ED) WORDS

A letter to others from Dan

> Dear Friends, Family, Colleagues and Loved Ones,
>
> I want to tell you a story that has been a bit of a joke among some close staff members.
>
> As I was leaving India after a pretty hard event where we had an amazing facilitation team, I was walking through the airport with Bob. Bob spent much of his week exploring the possibilities of working on a full-time level with Wycliffe Associates. He is a great guy who truly loves people and pours his heart and soul into them. He has worked in some of the toughest places on the planet and loves it because of the people.
>
> When we were leaving, he said something like, "I don't know how you do this, it just breaks me up inside to leave these people after an event..." I was passively listening as I watched where to go in the airport and I passively answered, "yeah...I know..." And Bob stopped me. He said, "What did you say?!" He further went on to laugh at me and said, "No you don't! You don't care!" Half serious and half with humor, he was saying "you're busted," making fun of my non-emotion as I go from one event to the next all around the globe.
>
> That occurrence was funny. It had truth and I re-

alized I was pretty much able to do what he was saying. I am able to go from one event to the next and leave and move on. Perhaps it is the teacher in me when I would have to say goodbye to students after spending a year with them. Perhaps it was how I was wired, but Bob was right, I was "busted" for being far from his level of emotional expression.

We have shared this story for years now and it has many tentacles that paint me as missing my emotional genes to heartless (all joking and very funny between us). Yet, there is a different reality behind the deeply buried truth. It is one of love. To distinguish audience, I am writing to in this letter, let me be specific:

- The precious family that I leave behind much of the year

- The staff I lead and coworkers that I fight with in battle of doing this translation work

- The translators that I encounter briefly

- The national leaders whom I've planned with and learned from

- The Wycliffe Associates leaders who have trusted and supported me

I want you to know, I love you all. I would die for you. I would serve you. I would share your burdens. You have not only greatly impacted me, you have made me who I am and after God, none of this is possible without any of you.

When this is done and my last words are written, I want you to know that if I am remembered for anything, it should just be "a teacher". After that, the only discussion is the adjectives that describe what kind of teacher and those are all things that are from you.

Truly, thank you for the ability to write these words

and so many more that will never be seen by anyone but God.

With love, respect, joy and admiration,

Dan

M.A.S.T

Mobilized Assistance Supporting Translation

Brain-based Bible Translation Methodology

TABLE OF CONTENTS

Introducing a Translation Methodology in a 3.0 Paradigm

Foundation upon which the Theory is Built

B ible translation is both a sacred responsibility and a precious opportunity. It is a gift of God that He calls us to be part of spreading His truth to the nations. But it is also a calling to something immeasurably important. We cannot take this lightly. We must never ignore the sacred nature of our task. Yet, we cannot assume that this highest of all callings will be accomplished century after century by the same methods and principles. Certainly we can all agree that Wycliffe himself did not employ modern methods now espoused as essential to the production of a good translation. Nor did the team who was tasked with the King James Translation in 1619. Down through the centuries, methodologies have changed. Good translations have been produced taking copious amounts of time, but with minimal technology. Good translations have also been produced with the use of the most modern technology available. And, of course, poor translations have been produced, both because of a lack of commitment to the truth of God's Word, and a lack of essential effort. The bottom line is, in any translation effort, the ultimate

136

guide to the production of a true translation is depen-
dence upon the Holy Spirit and an unwavering commitment to the veracity of His Word. Scholarly debates on
issues of accuracy and transference of meaning versus
literal wording, will continue. We cannot allow ourselves to get bogged down by these disagreements.
Instead we must rely on God's power and His Spirit to
give us wisdom as we forge ahead. The MAST methodology is solidly founded on the belief that the Bible
is God's Holy Word, that God Himself is the agent for
getting His message to the world, and that we, His children, are uniquely designed and called by God to be
instruments in this process.

INTRODUCING MAST—MOBILIZED ASSISTANCE SUPPORTING TRANSLATION

We have it. We always have. The reality is, we have
always desired to resist The One who gave it to us in
the first place. At Babel, God said, "Come let us go
down and confuse their language so that they will not
understand each other." From that point in time, we can
see that God spoke toward the capacity of human functioning to deal with multiple languages. He did not put
us to sleep to change something in our brains or tongues;
nor did he start it in a future generation. Instead, in
Genesis 11 at Babel, He instantly used the human pre-
wired language brain and changed the course of history.
Science affirms human functioning of a pre-wired language (Chomsky 1965) brain through multiple tests that
now include monitoring of neurons (Lenneberg 1967)
starting as far back as Karl Wernicke (Boeree 2004).
Yet, while language functioning is one of the pre-set
human gifts, it is still one of the more complex elements

to fully pin-down as an accurate science of predict-ability. Language, although often attached to individual developmental traits of human learning (visual, audi-tory, kinesthetic), early brain theory (left/right brain), or even personality theory, we are still learning exactly how the brain takes in language, settles it, grows it and owns it as a tool (Bogen 1976). Despite the complexity, however, what we must acknowledge today is that each human (barring a neurological disadvantage) is born with the capacity to learn a language and use it in their surrounding environment.

Mobilized Assistance Supporting Translation (MAST) is a Bible Translation methodology that begins with the basis that all humans have language, and can use it to the fullest possible capacity of God-given ability. If Bible translation is a function of language (written or oral), then any human who possesses the ability to use their language also possess the ability to participate in Bible translation.

LINGUISTIC PRINCIPLES OR GRAMMAR-BASED THEORY?

Today, there are thousands of aspiring English teachers in college education programs that include "linguistic principles" for a variety of reasons. One of the primary reasons universities have decided to include linguistic courses in the curriculum of English teachers is due to the changes in the field of grammar and the impact that new theory could potentially have upon teaching (Lefevre 1965). Despite this inclusion of linguistics courses over the last 30 years, there has truly been little change to the nature of English teaching or the inclu-sion of linguistic theory. The reason is, as the trends

138

of linguistic theory emerged in curriculum, the "grammarians" noticed their funding and academic status changing. Soon grammarians began reshaping themselves to become the "new linguistics" educators of the field (McCauley 1980).

Nevertheless, the field of grammar study and the field of linguistic study is very different at the core. Despite the fact that both fields include language and thus have overlapped in educational study, debate, funding and research, ultimately, they differ.

The basic fundamental principles of grammar theory are as follows (Newmayer 1988, Fatima 1999, Robins 1967):

1. There is an internal set of rules in language shared by speakers.
2. There is a conscious attempt to define rules.
3. There is an analysis of language through de-contextualizing parts of speech (in any form).
4. There is a "proper language".
5. Vocabulary is for meta-linguistic discussion (vocabulary has a context).
6. Language is broken into phonology, morphology, syntax and pragmatic functioning.

In Contrast, fundamental principles of linguistic theory are as follows:

1. Children learn language swiftly, efficiently and without instruction.
2. Language operates by rules.
3. All languages have sound, vocabulary and grammar.
4. Everyone has dialect.
5. There is style, sub-dialect and slang in language.
6. Language is connected to society.

7. Value judgments about language is prefer-ence-based only.
8. Writing is connected to speech.

Someone could look at these two sets of traits and say on the surface, "they agree" or "they are similar" or "they assist one another"; they might—until you try to use the function of one field within another.

Consider the following example: You are going to teach the writing of an essay. A grammar-based meth-odology would have you do the following:

1. Analyze, outline and gather information in the form of vocabulary.
2. Structure your writing in a way to the proper language of the target audience.
3. Express the rules in as much detail as you can before (and even interrupting within to keep things "in-context", often through "mini-lessons")

Again, in contrast, a linguistic view would approach the same assignment in the following way:

1. Consider how you would discuss this concept of your essay with someone and think about it.
2. Write it, write it quickly, naturally and without worry.
3. Keep your target audience in mind
4. Don't worry—produce.

The learner who is writing the essay would undoubtedly see a difference between the structures of the two ways in which to produce an essay. This is also true of Bible translation methodology. At the core, which methodology is truly being applied—is it grammar-based functioning, linguistic, or a hybrid of "whatever works"?

MAST methodology starts with a core of linguistic-based principles that are carried out to the extreme end of leaving grammar-based functioning well behind. The reasoning behind the pull-away from any grammar-based theory is not because of past paradigm, but rather because of the bleak educational research that has been done on the use of grammatical teaching principles in impact upon any function of language (reading, writing, speaking, listening, foreign language). In short, over a hundred years of condensed research (Weaver 1996), there are decades of research showing negative impact on language use in an educational setting (McCaulley et al 1980). Linguistic principles applied to a language-based education approach is the first framing guideline to understanding MAST methodology. If you understand the above principles and how they impact language usage as "do" vs "start by understanding" you are ready to begin applying each layer of educational theory that feeds into how a human with language can use their ability to begin translation.

THE FOUNDATIONAL BASE FOR AN MTT— AUTHENTIC ASSESSMENT AND JUST IN TIME LEARNING

Imagine a 3rd grade classroom that started with the statement "We're sorry, we are only going to accept students who have the ability to perform calculus. We know this is a high expectation for your age, but this is all we are equipped to do." Now imagine that same statement in a private school that has to function from a certain budget in order to survive. How would they do as a system? I

141

would not only worry for that school, I would worry for that community in need of a school. Frankly, I would worry for that classroom full of third grade students as well. As for an education system, this would be failure.

MAST methodology is based upon education system reality—"this is what you get to work with." No longer can you tell a person with language that you must also have a second language (gateway), a third language that would really help (English), Biblical background to the point of exegetical understanding, academic literacy at a college level (or more), computer literacy, and if you're really skilled some extra-Biblical languages. Instead, now imagine that you must accept anyone into your classroom.

The concept of authentic assessment is to take a real person, in real-time, with a real glimpse of skill (Gabriela, Sweet 2000). Once that skill is identified, we then understand what we can/cannot do and move forward. In the case of Bible translation, the ideal world may have some of the above skills (maybe even more) mentioned. However, what if those skills could be removed? What if their minimum stage to contribute was simply their language functioning?

- The skills of MAST are the following:
- Do you have first language fluency in reading, writing, speaking, listening, academic understanding?
- Do you have national/gateway language fluency in reading, writing, speaking, listening, academic understanding?
- What is your level of thinking skill that is comfortable for you? (Blooms Taxonomy/Brain Theory shared in the theory breakdown of this document)

- What is your level of Biblical knowledge?
- What is the level of computer literacy?
- What is your personality style and preference of learning?

Authentic Assessment

MAST begins with authentic assessment of individuals according to the above skills set (see appendix A). After this, begins the path of inclusion of participants (versus exclusion), remembering the linguistic principles. These principles, summarized by "just do" (versus start by understanding), cut off years of training, development and front-loaded information that never transfers satisfactorily (Wagner 1970).

Authentic assessment begins by focusing on the end-goal. The desired skills in their fullest form are listed. After generating that list, each is defined by either "sub-lists" or holistic paragraph descriptions. Once the skill list is developed, the decision can be made regarding how to measure that skill in as natural an environment as possible. Upon observance, one can rank each skill on a Likert 5 point scale. At this point the skills measured are collected and and the learners are grouped accordingly to their skill level and the groupings that function within the goals desired.

Just In-Time

Despite the "just do" belief system and the desire to remove the years of training, we do not propose an absence of training. We can all acknowledge the value of good internship experiences. Nothing expresses this quite like some practices in the medical field that go by an underlying principle "see one, do one, teach one." How nervous does it make you feel when you read the word "one"? I know I would personally like my doctor to have several, if not hundreds of attempts at something before I am in-line for surgery.

We all know before even the "see one" there is hours of classroom experience, reading, exams, experiments, practice, and study, that make up instructional time. Truly, it could be said, "learn, see, do, teach." Now imagine the absence of the "see" and "do" as applied to the medical field. Suddenly, I will take the "one" back in the "see one, do one, teach one" scenario. Edgar Dale expresses the power of instruction, versus seeing, versus doing in his cone of experience. (see diagram at: http://www.educ.ualberta.ca/staff/olenka.Bilash/best%20of%20bilash/dalescone.html) Through his work, we can see that each teaching/learning activity that is a part of instruction has an impact upon memory. Thus, retention can be manipulated based upon what learners (in this case, translators) are asked to do in their functioning (ie—the process of translation). We understand the difference in brain impact (memory functioning) from reading (20 percent retention) to doing the real thing (80-90 percent retention). Apply this to teaching the core principles of Bible translation in an instructional environment versus a "doing" environment.

Let's go back to the 3rd grade classroom. If all of those students were assessed on their math skills and regardless of where they were you had to take them into the classroom, authentic assessment will do a good job of identifying individuals in skill and further grouping them for goals. After they are grouped, imagine creating experiences for those students based upon their ability. Those experiences walk them through the steps of achievement. Further, those experiences surround them with context, other learners (who have a variety of skills) and create a community of learners that assist in the cultivation of exposure to needed outcomes. Not only is the forum for teaching needed principles set, the forum for identifying others who have the skills to point to are surrounding you.

There are countless fields that implement this model of instruction whether identified or not. Some of these concepts can be found in pilot training schools, medical facilities, manufacturing jobs, and marketing arenas. The question is no longer "How quickly can we teach skills as we go?" the question is "What skill is not teachable within a context of doing?" (Wind and Reibstein 2000)

The day of pre-loading information before you can start a task is quickly disappearing. To believe that it is the most effective way of training has long since been abandoned by effective dynamic systems. Using authentic assessment to identify "what we have" and then setting the job out with teaching context surrounding those in the task "as they go" is the second principle to MAST.

EDUCATIONAL STAPLES CROSSING ALL PROCESS METHODOLOGY

After the foundation of linguistic understanding and the assessment of learners within the context of just-in-time learning, there are learning principles that should always be applied to translation methodology. These principles are affirmed through educational practices of good teaching, as well as, good practice in educational treatment of language process. The following is a list of educational theories that are used within MAST process throughout all the steps:

Least Restrictive Environment Theory—removing as many barriers as possible for the translator to do their job without interruption. The theory originated through a United States federal entitlement that required educational systems to teach students with disabilities in regular classrooms as much as is possible to maximizes a child's ability to receive maximum educational benefits while participating in a regular educational environment as much as possible. The policy includes the inclusion of elements of individualized instruction that requires the educational system/teacher to view the individual based upon their authentic educational realities (Meador 2014).

Individualized Instruction—pulling from multiple intelligence learning theory and psychology personality theory, the ways in which individuals best learn vary according to who they are, how they think and to some extent, what their preferences are. An example could be (but is not limited to) Gardner's multiple intelligence theory that breaks learning into seven modalities including: musical–rhythmic, visual–spatial, verbal–linguistic, logical–mathematical, bodily–kinesthetic, interpersonal, intra-personal, and naturalistic (Gardner 1993). Other theories that might be used for teams include: Shapes personality theory by Connie Podesta, Left-Right Brain Theory, Continuum Theories of Personality (varied approaches), True Colors by Don Lowry, etc. The basic principles applied to MAST methodology is to see each individual in the process and adapt the learning/teaching/drafting/checking steps to the strength of the individual. Likewise, adapt the methodology to the weakness of the individual.

Value-based Learning—from a combination of counseling methodology, psychology research and education theory, we have learned that there are certain factors in human existence that inspire people toward motivation, leading to higher performance in their work. Well-known professionals in the field of marriage counseling and relationships, such as Dr. Gary Smalley and Dr. Kevin Leman, as well as, certain highly regarded research organizations, such as The Search Institute (The Assets), demonstrate some of the common characteristics in humans that express a sense of value in individuals. If we can use these characteristics (such as feedback, praise, decision-making, ownership, and voice, to name a few) and attach them to the work that translators are doing, the sense of motivation increases.

Ownership/Motivation—the concept that the individual is best motivated through their ownership, control of task and completion of the work. Ownership principles base their core in constructivist education. This theory focuses upon larger tasks that are life related and the components of the work are in context to this task goal. The individuals have a time of feeling supported but quickly transition to self-motivated control of the task. The tasks are authentic and are adjusted to the participant. Reflection is a regular part of ownership. Facilitation should allow and encourage ideas, different views, and even different contexts-(De Lisi 2002)

147

Scaffolding—the concept that layers of learning build upon and upward to more layers of learning. Lev Vygotsky and Jerome Bruner developed approaches to learning that today have been coined as "scaffolding". The concept is to provide resources within a task. As the task is demonstrating understanding, the resources (or facilitators) can be removed and/or reduced. At that point, the one within the task is able to build context integrating skill to the next level of use. (Vygotsky 1986).

Time Principles of Brain-based education—time is an impacting element of education and writing process. Basic time principles today point toward processing first time information in a limited time span (5-7 minutes in a chunk), and working with information in a limited time span (7-11 minutes in a chunk). Once these time parameters are broken, long-term-memory function (and to some extent, short-term as well) is reduced from full functionality. (Sousa 2011)

People rise to the level of expectation—by providing the platform of high standard and expectation, people accelerate their efforts, increasingly accelerating their output (Cotton 1989).

THE PROCESS—NOT THE SAME OLD THING

Theory, methods and planning are three elements of educational process. Theory is the research arm of experimentation that gives validation to methods. Methods are the core elements that give educators the freedom to teach. Planning is the specific approach to a particular audience. Over time, these three elements seem to have morphed in many education systems into a systemic exposure to information. It's not that exposure to information is bad, but without theory, methods and planning, the reality of impact is significantly reduced. In turn, whenever a process is given that does not continue to maintain the methodology core (that also points back to theoretical foundation), the process itself becomes detached from the performers (students).

Good methodology lends to flexibility. Good methodology points back to theory. Good theory is based on research over time in relationship to the human-centered reaction. Once we remove good methodology and/or take a process removed from the methodology and treat it as "good process" without the ability to be altered, we have now moved the target of output from person centered to process centered. MAST attempts to remain in a state of methodology with process that is adaptable to the collective individuals who are engaging in translation. This lends to a constant flow of the pieces of the process in order, time, usage and treatment within each step. Simply put, the translator is at the center of the translation, not the process.

The MAST methodology process steps are as follows:

- Worship, Prayer and focus time
- Reading of text
- Discussion of text (outlines, exegetical review, key word exposure)
- Blind Drafting
- Individual Critique
- Peer Review
- Church Review
- Keyword Check
- Consultant Check

- Community Check

- (Editing steps throughout)
- Back Translation as desired/where desired

While all of these steps could look familiar to much or all of the traditional translation process in wording/ concept, the theoretical base of linguistics (vs grammar analysis) changes how they play out in form. The educational treatments (above) also play into each of the steps making them look very different from traditional practice. Further, the theoretical base behind each one is constantly pushing against all of the steps and lends to the flexibility of each step within. Below are the theories related to each step:

- Worship, Prayer and focus time
  - Acts 2, honoring God with language
  - Praise/Encouragement/Feedback is given during this time each day offering motivational learning theory cues.
  - Time initiated brain activity applied as learners need to "warm-up" their thinking brain. Performance best happens after a short time of instruction (vs immediately jumping in). This sequence allows the discussion of text/drafting time to be the highest level of brain functioning.

- Reading of text
  - Sustained-Silent Reading Principles applied—the reader best interacts with text
  - Literature Circles Theory Applied

- Discussion of text (outlines, exegetical review, key word exposure)
  - Higher Level Thinking (Bloom)
  - Scaffolding (Vygotsky) for layering in key words that build throughout the day (vs a front loading of information expecting it to transfer into context of translation)
  - Ownership theory (through the taking of content into their own schema)
  - Bilingual language layers of discussion to form initial cross referencing of content in language.

- Blind Drafting/Chunking of text
  - Chunking text into the largest manageable pieces for "retelling" (writing) in target language.
  - Closing the source text to rely on memory for naturalness, speed and removing a grammar translation process of language approach.
  - Comprehensible output of language (input hypothesis + output hypothesis)

- Individual Critique
  - Editing Technique (Atwell)
    - Time—spend time in your writing
    - Ownership—control the direction of the writing and reflect upon it deeply
    - Response—-reflect upon improvements in designated forms (instructional input)

  - Error Correction
    - Treat vs Delay—the conscious effort to correct or wait

- ■Transfer Treatment—the conscious choice to seek help
  - ■ Treat versus ignore—identify the concept as minimal to comprehension (ie—preference)
  - ■ Diagnostic—use a rubric of skills to identify potential errors

- Peer Review
  - ○ Process Editing (technique driven)
  - ○ Textual comparison (usually gateway language—known in some circles as content checking.)

- Church Review
  - ○ Direct translation standards applied (clarity, naturalness, accuracy)

- Keyword Check
  - ○ Vocabulary study (is it there?)
  - ○ Consistency measurement (have we seen this elsewhere?)
  - ○ Comprehension Check (are they understood?)

- Consultant Check
  - ○ Tradition Consultants Used
  - ○ Content Centered Language Checking—the context of language "holds itself" in a container creating boundaries of meaning.

- Community Check
  - ○ Large group literature circle process (with editing process)

       ° Keyword checking process applied large scale

       ° Church Review process applied

- (Editing steps throughout)
- Back Translation as desired/where desired

THE FLEXIBILITY OF THEORY AND METHODS

There are three primary models for the MAST program:

- Two Week Model: If there is a church that can mobilize 26 members of one language, MAST process can take on a New Testament translation in two weeks with all of the same above steps.
- 40 Week Model: If there are several language groups (of 2-3 members each) that can work in a cluster, MAST process can implement a New Testament timeline of 40 weeks until completion.
- Oral Language MAST: if there is a group with no developed orthography or even mother-tongue literacy, MAST can be implement in either the two week or 40 week model.

While there is a core of steps listed, they are fluid in sequence within the steps, and offer the ability to take in more. Whereas one group may have a church check, for others that could easily merge into a larger community check. Some variations within the steps include:

- Order of steps—the ability to change, integrate or even exclude/delay steps. This could include a variety of sequences in the checking steps,

153

groups working at different speeds (as individuals fragment onto different tasks), etc.

- Order of "pieces" within steps—the ability to change, condense, expand parts of steps within the MAST process. For example, within the "reading" step of the methodology, it could include reading, discussion, exegetical overview, keyword discussion. These steps could happen in any order as needed by the group facilitator.

- Inclusion of identified needs/special requests— the ability to add more layers of checking (back translation), layers of Greek/Hebrew checking, inclusion of more exegetical resources, directed approach to editing for specific language groups, increased discussion of keywords due to dialect discrepancy, etc.

- Inclusion of tools/technology-based functioning—at any step in the process, technology-based and/or partner-based tools can be implemented at any time.

THEORETICAL BREAKDOWN OF STEPS

The above lists the steps in functionality/flow; the following lists the "eye on theory". While this is not something that needs to be "front and center" for everyone participating in a MAST, it needs to be pointed toward so the adjustments and flexibility remain sound and based upon theoretical principles.

- Assessment
  - ○ Authentic Assessment Principles: measuring the translators based upon a contextualized, authentic, task-based, learner-centered task in real time with simulated purpose for skills measurement. (Sweet)
  - ○ Left Brain/Right Brain Theory: measuring the translators based upon more creative versus analytical based thinking patterns (through authentic assessment)
  - ○ Blooms Higher Level Thinking: Framing contextual questions that seek answers which identify translators within thinking skill level.
  - ○ CALP (Cognitive Academic Language Performance): Identifying academic reading/thinking response to varying degrees of (Biblical) content (Cummins 2007).

- Worship, Prayer and focus time
  - ○ David Sousa/Brain Theory of Time
  - ○ Motivational Theory of Piaget Constructivism with parameters of support, scaffolding (Vygotsky) and value traits (Search Institute).

- Reading of text
  - ○ Sustained Silent Reading: The implementation of reading during a brain-based active time (1-2 hours after breakfast/wake-up time), in a least-restrictive environment setting (relaxed and stress free) with modeled facilitation. (Krashen 2011)
  - ○ Brain Theory—time of day (Sousa)

- Discussion of text (outlines, exegetical review, key word exposure)
    - ○ Literature Circles: The use of guided discussion in natural, higher level thinking questions (Bloom) that direct small groups towards ownership of text orally. (Storm 2014)

- Blind Drafting
    - ○ Chunking/Heaps and Complexes: The concept of taking complete chunks of thought (heap) and merging them with other chunks of thought (complexes) in context to build schema and contextual language output (Vygotsky)
    - ○ Writing in-context: (Atwell 1998, Sheridan 2000)

- Individual Critique
    - ○ The Writing Lab: A semi-structured environment where writers feel safe and free to explore their own context of writing through the process of editing that is prompted by the facilitator in simple steps, but controlled by the writer in correction. (Atwell)

- Peer Review
    - ○ Editing Process: structured time for focused revision with elements of specific analysis looked at ranging from purely identified editing skills, content formation (exegetical correctness) to standards of output (Translation Standards).

○ Error Correction: The formal process of focusing on errors based upon the facilitator's identification of individual error.

○ Zone of Proximal Development (ZPD)/ Monitor Theory: The ZPD (Vygotsky) and monitor theory of language development (Krashen 1982) places individuals in a learning context that surrounds them with others who have differing skill sets. Upon the internal identification of these skills, the motivation to acquire new skills and/or natural gleaning of these skills from interrelated work increases the output, potential and overall task motivation.

- Church Review
  ○ Editing Process/Error Correction repeated with Translation Measurements applied

- Keyword Check
  ○ Vocabulary comprehension check to first identify the existence of key terms, then the consistency and then the overall comprehension (Scaffolding).

- Consultant Check
  ○ Teacher Training Transfer: The consultant check in MAST process has two goals— to check the accuracy and to take the steps of checking into a teaching process that begins to train nationals to assist and eventually take over the job of checking. Understanding this is a highly functioning

157

set of skills, the current model of practice in doing this is still surrounded by consultants.

- Community Check
  - ○ Literature Circle/Editing Process/Error Correction Process Applied

INTERSECTING ROADS IN WA PROGRAMMING

MAST is a methodology that even if perfect (and it is not) and could take on the entire scope of translation through the mobilization of people, that is not the long-range goal, nor a goal in isolation. MAST is a tool within 3.0 paradigm that aligns with all of the other emerging elements we can currently identify. The larger goal of this paradigm is to enable the church to not only use paradigm 3.0 tools today, but well into the future beyond the scope of the current work.

Currently, here is how MAST functions with other WA related 3.0 paradigm pieces:

Translation Studio Through the development of notes and gateway language scripture, MAST is merging the methodology to function with translation studio tools so that anyone anywhere can use these tools together through technology-based resources.

Door 43/Open Bible Stories (OBS) MAST is fully capable and in alignment with the translation of OBS, Translation Notes, Gateway Language Scripture and/or minority language scripture translation. The church is in sole possession of what material is to be translated

158

and MAST provides the methodology to translate that material.

Open-source Publishing MAST is fully in alignment with translated materials being open-sourced materials.

Computer Aided Translation Currently, MAST has not yet attempted a "merged" methodology with computer aided programs (such as Sovee), but is attempting to do so in the first quarter of 2015.

What We Have Witnessed

June 2014

- Four seasoned translation teams applied MAST methodology to I and II Thessalonians in 5 days with an additional two days consultant checking, after which both books were ready to be taken back to the respective churches for final checking.
- One completely new team to translation completed I Thessalonians with consultant checking in 5 days.

Feedback from June workshop:
- Two consultants—one checked every verse and testified to quality translations. The second checked a variety of passages (1 full chapter of I Thessalonians in the new group and sat in on a full chapter of the other four languages assisting in the consultation) with positive feedback to the work.

159

- The partner/requesting organization with 15 years of organizational translation experience attested to the quality of the translation.
- The community feedback to the translation work taken back to the people was positive.
- The specific translators (who struggled in the early stages of the methodology) all attested to the positive results and have continued to use it verbally expressing an increase in pace of translating while still going through consultant checking of traditional measures.
- The new group gathered and requested to mobilize their churches for more work through the pastors who saw the work in their community.

November 2014

Two language groups with no translation experience, no written text and no first language literacy were gathered. In six days, group "L" translated one Open Bible Story (OBS), 8 stories for evangelism purposes and the book of Jonah. They further recorded their stories. The "M" group translated one OBS and the book of Philippians (and recorded both). Both groups made plans to continue the work, check it among community members and to gather together again to give feedback and check some more work. The work of both groups was consultant checked.

November 2014

The "new" group as mentioned above gathered their community together to attempt to complete an entire New Testament in two weeks (See Appendix B timetable/distribution). The community did not have the 26 people gathered, but instead gathered 14. With two consultants present, the group drafted and checked all four gospels and I and II Timothy (somewhere between 48-49.8% depending on how you calculate). The group has appointed a translation committee, the supporting organization had committed to further working on orthography/dialect issues detected (as well as other editing needs) and the gathered group has committed to exposing the text to the community over several months until they gather again to complete the second half of the New Testament.

The program is young. The program is beginning to grow in partnership in a variety of levels, but most importantly, with the church. While young, we can attest to the current level of satisfaction in the drafting process, the naturalness and the speed from all partners involved. As well, every partner has been "impressed" with the ability to take non-trained translators and implement them to a level of drafting that is clearly workable up to the point of consultant checking. Every MAST experience to-date has had consultants present and the MAST program is committed to upholding these standards so that the church can have the ability to implement naturalness, clarity, accuracy and reliability of text in a transfer of skills.

ELIJAH MOMENTS

Beyond the theory, the critique and the attempts, it needs to be understood that MAST is an endeavor of faith. We know what statements such as "two weeks to a New Testament" look like to the translation world. All the same, there is no lack of precedent in faith statements

161

in Scripture. How ridiculous was it for Elijah to call together an audience of 850 critics, rebuild a torn down altar, drench it in water and after hours of the oppressors seeing nothing happen, to call upon God for fire to consume his offering? Elijah set the stage. We need to as well, because Elijah's God is our God and if we never set the stage, how can He possibly show up? He is the agent and we are His chosen instruments. His Word is a sacred message meant for the people of the world. This is our bold belief. This is our faith statement. The stage is set and MAST is seeking bold miracles.

Appendix A

Authentic Assessment Example for Grouping MTTs According to Skills

Skills Assessment

Divide the students into evenly distributed groups. Each assessor, have a sheet of paper, write your area of assessment and your name at the top of the page. For each student, write their name and their score.

Each rotation will last about 10 minutes or less.

Each assessment will be scored on a scale of 1-5 with one being the lowest level and five the highest.

1. Station 1: Have the students do the following:
   a. Read a 5 verse selection from scripture that does not focus on proper names or complex analogies. Rate (on scale of 1-5) their level of smoothness and clarity. Second, ask them two key questions about the passage (one knowledge question—"where is, who is, what is…." And one comprehension question—"how did, what does it mean….") and rate their ability to answer you.
   b. Tell the students to introduce themselves with three things about themselves. After, have the students write down something

about the other student In their mother-tongue. Rate both their oral and written responses.

2. Station 2: English Fluency
    a. Read a 5 verse selection from Scripture that does not focus on proper names or complex analogies. Rate their level of smoothness and clarity (rate 1 low to 5 high). Second, ask them two key questions about the passage (one knowledge question—"where is, who is, what is...." And one comprehension question—"how did, what does it mean....") and rate their ability to answer you in English.
    b. Tell the students to each introduce themselves in English with three things about themselves. After, have the students write down something about the other student in English. Rate both their oral and written responses.

3. Station 3: Mother Tongue Fluency (The lead should be our translator from last time unless we know of someone better.)
    a. Read a 5 verse selection from Scripture that does not focus on proper names or complex analogies. Rate their level of smoothness and clarity (rate 1 low to 5 high). Second, ask them two key questions about the passage (one knowledge question—"where is, who is, what is...." And one comprehension question—"how did, what does it mean....") and rate their ability to answer you.

    b. Tell the students to each introduce them-
selves in their mother-tongue with three
things about themselves. After, have the
students write down something about the
other student in their mother-tongue rate
both their oral and written response.

4. Station 4: Thinking Skill level
    a. Ask the learner to spin around in a 360
degree circle—which way do they spin—
left or right?
    b. Ask the leaner which traits best describe them.

LEFT BRAIN FUNCTIONS	RIGHT BRAIN FUNCTIONS
uses logic	uses feeling
detail oriented	"big picture" oriented
facts rule	imagination rules
words and language	symbols and images
present and past	present and future
math and science	philosophy & religion
can comprehend	can "get it" (i.e. meaning)
knowing	believes
acknowledges	appreciates
order/pattern perception	spatial perception
knows object name	knows object function
reality based	fantasy based
forms strategies	presents possibilities
practical	impetuous

ASK THE LEARNER TO IDENTIFY WHICH PICTURE ITEMS BEST DESCRIBE THEM? AND/OR WHICH SIDE OF THE BRAIN FITS THEM BETTER?

Is the student left brained or right brained?

Ask the students which of the four shapes they are? Triangle, Square, Circle, Squiggle (you can draw these shapes on the page)

Ask the student these two questions while you hold up a pencil or pen:

1. What is this? (if they say something simple, mark them an A, if they say something besides naming the item, like "it's an instrument for recording" then mark them a B)

2. What would you like to say about it? (if they say something simple, mark them an A, if they say something about how it impacts/changes things, or if they compare it to something, or if they talk about how it could be improved, mark them a B.)

5. Station 5: Biblical familiarity

   a. Ask the student how they would rate themselves on knowing/studying the Bible, 1 low to 5 high. Write their score down.

   b. Ask the student if they can name the books of the New Testament to you? Write down YES/NO

   c. Ask the student if they can tell you who wrote Romans, Revelation, Hebrews? If they can accurately name all 3, mark YES if not NO.

      d. Ask the student what their favorite book is? Write it down.

6. Station 6: Computer familiarity— WA Facilitator should lead this and can have a national assistant

      a. Have the student turn on the computer/tablet.

      b. Have the student follow your verbal directions to open the app. Rate their ability to do these first two steps using the 1 to 5 scale.

      c. Have the student type three sentences in the app (in any language). Rate their typing ability.

      d. Coding of Name Tags:

At the end of the assessments, the student name tags will be collected. Scripture is already divided in the following way: 1. "gospel half" and "the rest of the NT". 2. Level 1=Mark, Level 2=Luke, Level 3=Matthew, Level 4=John. 3. Within levels, daily distribution to each of the team members for the current chapter/chunks.

Level 1 = Yellow, Level 2 = Green, Level 3 = Red, Level 4 = Blue

C = Computer Literate

E = English

X = No national fluency or English

Translator	MT Fluency	Nat Fl	Eng Fl	Brain	Think	Tablet

Appendix B

Sample Scripture Distribution List and Order of Progression

Level 1=yellow, Level 2=green, Level 3=red, Level 4=Blue

Mark(678)Luke(1151)Matthew (1071)John (879)

Galatians (149)2 Corinthians (257)Acts (1007) Romans (437)

Ephesians (155)Titus (46)**Total (2078)**1 Corinthians (437)

Philippians (104)James (108)Hebrews (303)

Colossians (95)1 Peter (105)**Total (2048)**

2 Thessalonians (47)2 Peter (61)

1 Timothy (113)1 John (105)

2 Timothy (83)2 John (13)

Philemon (25)3 John (15)

Jude (25)**(Total 1886)**

Revelation (404)

Total (1874)

This will be assessed as we go and shuffled as monitored.

BIBLIOGRAPHY

Atwell, Nancie. (1998) <u>In the Middle: New Understandings About Writing, Reading, and Learning.</u> ISBN-13: 978-0867093742

Boeree, George C (2004) Speech and the Brain. http://www.ship.edu/cgboeree/speechbrain.html

Bogen JE, Bogen GM (1976). <u>"Wernicke's region—Where is it?"</u>. *Annals of the New York Academy of Sciences* **280**: 834–43.

Chomsky, N. *Aspects of the Theory of Syntax*. MIT Press, 1965. <u>ISBN 0-262-53007-4</u>.

Cotton, Kathleen. "Expectations and Student Outcomes." Portland, Oregon: Northwest Regional Educational Laboratory, November 1989. 18 pages.

Cummins, J., Brown, K., & Sayers, D. (2007). Literacy, technology, and diversity: Teaching for success in changing times. Boston: Allyn & Bacon.

Dale, E. (1969) Audiovisual methods in teaching, third edition. New York: The Dryden Press;

Holt, Rinehart and Winston.

De Lisi, R. (2002). From Marbles to Instant Messenger™ : Implications of Piaget's Ideas About Peer Learning. *Theory Into Practice*, 41(1), 5.

Fatima Sadiqi, Moha Ennaji.(1999).<u>Introduction To Modern Linguistics</u>. Afrique-Orient.

Krashen, Stephen D., 2011. *Free Voluntary Reading*. Santa Barbara: Libraries Unlimited, chapter 1

Krashen, S. (1982). *Principles and practice in second language acquisition*. Oxford: Pergamon Press

Lefevre, Carl A (1965) Contributions of Linguistics to Teacher Education Programs. Chicago, IL. National Council of Teachers of English.

Lehman, Kevin (2006) The <u>Birth Order Book.</u> Grand Rapids, MI. Baker Publishing.

Lenneberg, Eric H (1967) Biological Foundations of Language. New York City.

Lyons, J. (1981). *Language and Linguistics*. Cambridge: Cambridge University Press.

McCawley, J.D. 1980. Review of Newmeyer, F. (1980) Linguistic theory in America: the first quarter-century of transformational

Meador, Derrick. (2014) An Overview of the Individuals with Disabilities Educational Act. About Education. http://teaching.about.com/od/law/a/Individuals-With-Disabilities-Education-Act.htm

Newmeyer, FJ. (ed.) (1988) <u>Linguistics: The Cambridge Survey</u>. Cambridge: C.U.P.

Robins, R.H.(1967). A short History of Linguistics. London: Longmans.

Sheridan, Daniel (2000) Teaching Secondary English: Reading and Applications. ISBN-13: 978-0805828719

Smalley, Gary and Trent, John (1988). The language of love : a powerful way to maximize insight, intimacy, and understanding. Pomona, Calif. : Focus on the Family Pub. ; Waco, Tex. : Distributed by Word Books

Sousa, David A. (2011). How the Brain Learns. ISBN-13: 978-1412997973

Storm, Lisa. (2014) Literacture Circles: Getting Started. Urbana, IL. NCTE http://www.readwritethink.org/classroom-resources/lesson-plans/literature-circles-getting-started-19.html

Sweet, Gabriela, Reed, David, Lutz, Ursula, Alegia, Cheryl. (2000). Developing Speaking and Writing Tasks for 2nd Language Assessment. Minnesota. Center for Advanced Research on Language Acquisition.

The Search Institute (2014). Developmental Assets: Preparing the Young for Success. http://www.search-institute.org/what-we-study/developmental-assets

Vygotsky, Lev. (1986) Thought and Language. ISBN-13: 978-0262720106

Wagner, Robert W. Edgar Dale: Professional. Theory into Practice. Vol. 9, No. 2, Edgar Dale (Apr., 1970), pp. 89-95

Weaver, Constance. (1996) Teaching Grammar in Context. Miami. Heinneman.

Wild, Jerry and Reibstein, David. (2000) Just-in-time Education: Learning in the Global Information Age. Knowledge and Wharton. http://knowledge. wharton.upenn.edu/article/just-in-time-education-learning-in-the-global-information-age/

CPSIA information can be obtained
at www.ICGtesting.com
Printed in the USA
LVHW071621051020
667984LV00026B/4707